CONSTELLATIONS

Like the future itself, the imaginative possibilities of science fiction are limitless. And the very development of cinema is inextricably linked to the genre, which, from the earliest depictions of space travel and the robots of silent cinema to the immersive 3D wonders of contemporary blockbusters, has continually pushed at the boundaries. **Constellations** provides a unique opportunity for writers to share their passion for science fiction cinema in a book-length format, each title devoted to a significant film from the genre. Writers place their chosen film in a variety of contexts – generic, institutional, social, historical – enabling **Constellations** to map the terrain of science fiction cinema from the past to the present... and the future.

'This stunning, sharp series of books fills a real need for authoritative, compact studies of key science fiction films. Written in a direct and accessible style by some of the top critics in the field, brilliantly designed, lavishly illustrated and set in a very modern typeface that really shows off the text to best advantage, the volumes in the **Constellations** series promise to set the standard for SF film studies in the 21st century.'
Wheeler Winston Dixon, Ryan Professor of Film Studies, University of Nebraska

 Constellations

@Constelbooks

Also available in this series

Blade Runner Sean Redmond

Inception David Carter

Forthcoming

Altered States John Edmond

Robocop Omar Ahmed

Seconds Jez Conolly

These are the Damned Nick Riddle

CONSTELLATIONS

Close Encounters of the Third Kind

Jon Towlson

Acknowledgments

Special thanks to John Atkinson at Auteur for allowing this star child to go abroad, and for navigating the spacecraft so skilfully; and to my wife, Joanne Rudling, for taking the journey with me. Thanks to staff at the University of Texas; staff at The Brynmor Jones Library, University at Hull; and staff at the BFI Reuben Library, London Southbank, for access to resources and archive material. Thanks also to Mike Hawks at The Larry Edmunds Bookshop, Hollywood, for sourcing promotional material from the film's 1977 release.

First published in 2016 by
Auteur, 24 Hartwell Crescent, Leighton Buzzard LU7 1NP
www.auteur.co.uk
Copyright © Auteur 2016

Series design: Nikki Hamlett at Cassels Design
Set by Cassels Design www.casselsdesign.co.uk
Printed and bound by CPI Group (UK) Ltd, Croydon, CR0 4YY

British Library Cataloguing-in-Publication Data
A catalogue record for this book is available from the British Library

ISBN paperback: 978-1-911325-07-9
ISBN ebook: 978-1-911325-08-6

Contents

Poster for the original 1977 theatrical release.

Introduction: 'The UFOs Are Coming!'

November 21, 1977. *Newsweek* magazine announces in bold letters, 'THE UFOs ARE COMING!' On its cover, Spielberg's giant Mothership hovers over America's first national monument, Devil's Tower. Inside, there's an extensive (four page) review by Jack Kroll, accompanied by a profile of Spielberg and a feature on the UFO phenomenon that inspired the film. 'Fifteen million Americans can't be wrong, can they?' asks Kroll (that's the number of people in the United States who, at the time of Kroll's writing, say they have seen a UFO; included amongst them is the then-president, Jimmy Carter). 'If you're looking for a genuine mass experience of the late 1970s,' Kroll goes on, 'the baffling but insistent UFO phenomenon is undoubtedly the most extraordinary... that's what makes *Close Encounters of the Third Kind* a genuine work of the popular imagination. It's the first truly populist science fiction film' (1977: 88).

Arguable though this last statement may be (what about *Star Wars*?), what is so striking about Kroll's review of *Close Encounters* is that it demonstrates how so many of the political criticisms surrounding the film stem from the time of its initial reception, and how its cultural denotation as 'transcendent' science fiction was immediately recognised and accepted by some – but not all – critics.

The giant Mothership in Close Encounters.

A Hymn to Regression and Emotional Retardation

'It's a shame that a film as wide-eyed and sweet-tempered as this had to get all fouled up with the money-making miasma that currently affects the movie business,' Kroll proclaims early in his review, citing the David Begelman affair, in which the chief of Columbia Pictures at the time of *Close Encounters*' release was forced to resign due to financial irregularities, and the stock market panic that ensued after New York financial critic William Flanagan attended the Dallas premiere of the film and gave it a pan, as evidence of said miasma (1977: 88).

Reflecting on the Begelman fiasco in his book *The Hollywood Studio System*, Douglas Gomery remarks that 'while the grosses and profits of *Close Encounters* overwhelmed any losses from the Begelman embezzlements, at the time the press from outside Hollywood focussed only on the scandals' (2005: 281). And Kroll reveals how investors worried by negative impact of Flanagan's review on Columbia's stock price had been 'jangling the phones of film critics, begging for personal critiques to guide their manoeuvres in Columbia stock.' It's no wonder that millions of people want desperately to believe in the reality of other worlds and other beings, Kroll concludes despairingly, 'free from the hype and heartlessness that increasingly affect this paranoid planet' (1977: 88-89).

At the heart of Kroll's misgivings is his objection to the Hollywood blockbuster, then a relatively new phenomenon. 'Blockbusters like Spielberg's own *Jaws*, which grossed a staggering $400 million and his friend George Lucas's *Star Wars*, which is threatening that record, have brought a kind of fiscal pornography into the film world,' Kroll laments (1977: 89). It is not hard to see, then, how concerns amongst film critics in 1977 about 'fiscal pornography' would turn into ideological diatribes against 'Reaganite entertainment' and its infantilising effect on audiences in the 1980s, as blockbusters took over cinema financially and culturally (Britton, 2009: 97-154; Wood, 2003: 144-167). *Close Encounters* has been subject to many such attacks since its release (writing in *New West* [December 5th, 1977], Stephen Farber, for example, describes the film as a 'hymn to regression and emotional retardation').

Thomas Doherty sees the juvenilisation of American movies as a process which began with teenpics in the 1950s, giving rise to the general adoption within the industry of 'The Peter Pan Syndrome' (2002: 128). By the 1980s, the 'Peter Pan Syndrome' had become, in the words of Robin Wood, the 'Spielberg-Lucas Syndrome':

> The success of the films (of Spielberg and Lucas) is only comprehensible when one assumes a widespread *desire* for regression to infantilism, a populace who wants to be constructed as mock children (2003: 147 original emphasis).

Wood attributes this wish to nuclear anxiety and a fear of fascism: a need 'to be reassured, to evade responsibility and thought' (2003: 149), and points to the male characters in Spielberg's films as embodiments of this desire for regression. Thus Roy Neary in *Close Encounters* is marked as a transitional figure between Chief Brody in *Jaws* (1975) and Elliott in *E.T.* (1982) in his gravitation toward the infantile, presexual male: 'as he falls under the influence of the extraterrestrial forces,' writes Wood, 'his behaviour becomes increasingly infantile' (2003: 158). Both Wood and Britton regard the film's key imagery as symbolic of Roy's infantilism:

> Given the dirt he deposits all over the house, one might see him as regressing to the pre-toilet training period (Wood, 2003: 158).

> (Roy Neary) demolishes the family home in order to build a monolithic, excremental totem phallus in the middle of the living room before retiring, at the end of the film, to the interior of the spaceship whose inhabitants, like E.T., are both phallic and fetal (Britton, 2009: 151).

Since the 1980s, advancing the regression thesis, other critics have offered similar psychoanalytical readings of *Close Encounters*. Andrew M. Gordon suggests that the film presents a symbolic 'fusion with the maternal transformational object', epitomised by Roy's (and by extension the audience's) obsessive search for UFOs, which is itself a quest for the transformational object, 'a pilgrimage that goes backwards from adulthood to infancy' (2008: 60); whilst Vivian Sobchack speaks of Roy Neary's 'intense and incompatible desire both to regain his lost patriarchal power and become a born-again child' (2004: 284).

It is not surprising, then, that critics have linked this desire for regression (and incompatible need to regain lost patriarchal power) to the film's sense of religious ecstasy and overtones of authoritarianism. Robert Entman and Francis Seymour label as fascist the film's attacks on 'liberal democratic governments', its 'nostalgia for the country's past days of glory', and its climax 'where people group around a hypnotic force, a repudiation of the intellect and a glorification of surrender and servitude' (1978: 3-6). Tony Williams goes further still, calling *Close Encounters* 'nothing less than a Disneyland version of *Triumph of the Will*' (1983: 23).

Without wishing to dispute these critics (many of whom I admire), at the same time one has to ask: what is being criticised – *Close Encounters* specifically, Steven Spielberg generally, or 'Reaganite entertainment' as a whole? Is *Close Encounters* being read on its own terms or as part of a wider attack on blockbuster cinema?

Close Encounters as 'transcendent' science fiction

'It's the last section that gives *Close Encounters* its historic place in movie entertainment', Jack Kroll proclaims in his *Newsweek* review. 'There are many surprises detonated during this film-within-a-film, but more important is the feeling generated by the impact of the unprecedented upon the familiar, a kind of cushioned trauma that's close, I think, to that grandiose old idea of the sublime' (1977: 92). Here Kroll identifies the quasi-religiosity detected by many critics in later years, scorned by some. Williams, for example, sees 'transcendence' within *Close Encounters* as expression of an immature yearning for the security of control by an authoritarian power (1983: 22-29). Hugh Ruppersberg concludes similarly that in *Close Encounters* and other modern science fiction films (*Star Wars, E.T., Starman* [1985]) the presence of an 'alien messiah' provides resolution in a world where solution seems impossible, where the 'only satisfactory way of addressing the world's problems is imaginative appeal to superhuman agencies (because) humanity itself is impotent, incompetent' (1990:32).

But the idea of ET as alien messiah has also been disputed in the case of *Close Encounters*. M. Keith Booker asserts that the film includes 'absolutely no overt expressions of religious belief, and the only higher power actually shown... is that represented by the aliens themselves' (2006: 134). Other critics argue that transcendence in Spielberg's film is philosophical rather than religious. Douglas E.

Cowan, a Professor of Religious Studies, states that *Close Encounters* 'points out in no uncertain terms how limited, how pedantic, are our terrestrial religious notions. Indeed, the only way to read it as a Christian allegory is to reject it as a possible scenario for first contact' (2010: 88). 'Rather than aliens being a metaphor for God, God becomes a metaphor for aliens,' writes cultural theorist, Elana Gomel. 'Fictional aliens are merely the shorthand we use to indicate what lies beyond the self-imposed boundaries of our humanity' (2014: 13, 28).

Jack Kroll, in fact, makes the claim that 'Spielberg's vision is a humanist one' (1977: 89). He describes *Close Encounters* as the antithesis of *2001: A Space Odyssey* (1968) in this respect. Kubrick's frosty brilliance, Kroll adjudges, 'clothed an elitist nihilism, a metaphysical disgust with the human species whose only chance was to hurl itself in the furthest reaches of outer space to be reborn as some Nietzchean super-mind sailing among the stars' (ibid). Instead, Kroll locates *Close Encounters* within a tradition of 1950s flying saucer movies: 'but stretches (their) scale and resonance with brilliant special effects until the film flares up into something approaching awe' (ibid). Certainly, if *Close Encounters* starts with that 'classic genre of the 1950s', as Kroll (and others) suggest, it follows the Liberal tradition (in international relations terms) of *It Came From Outer Space* (1953) and *The Day the Earth Stood Still* (1951), whilst most Cold War science fiction – *Invaders from Mars* (1953), *War of the Worlds* (1953), *This Island Earth* (1955), *Earth VS. The Flying Saucers* (1956) – spoke to underlying anti-Communist paranoia rather than to optimism for lasting peace and co-operation. Indeed, *Close Encounters* reversed the general trend within science fiction to show aliens as invaders intent on destroying humanity so they can claim the Earth as their own.

Close Encounters, then, is a UFO movie that 'covers in spirit the thirty years of the UFO controversy' (Combs, 2000: 31). Just as the 1950s flying saucer films drew on Kenneth Arnold, Roswell, Project MK-Ultra and 'little green men', *Close Encounters* arose from a resurgence of UFOlogy in the 1970s that coincided with the growth of New Age movements, mysticism, alien abduction cults and an increasing belief in conspiracy theories (Morton, 2007: 11-17). Robin Wood observes of UFOs and their appropriation by Hollywood:

They have a habit of turning up at convenient moments in modern history: in the 50s with the cold war and the fear of Communist infiltration, everyone saw hostile flying saucers, and Hollywood duly produced movies about them; at a period when (in the aftermath of Vietnam and Watergate) we need reassurance, Hollywood produces *nice* extraterrestrials. (2003: 160 original emphasis)

The underlying theme throughout, Wood suggests, is the acceptance/rejection of Otherness. Tony Shaw describes how *It Came from Outer Space* condemns America's paranoid fear of the Other and delivers instead the message that 'the "civilized" West might have more to learn from the Other Side – terrestrial and ET... than prevailing discourse would allow.' (2005: 134). Spielberg himself placed *Close Encounters* within a Liberal context when in 2007 he commented during an interview for Turner Classic Movies, 'if we can talk to aliens in *Close Encounters of the Third Kind* why not to the Reds in the Cold War.' Such statements link *Close Encounters* very closely to the 1950s science fiction movies as an allegory of international relations.

Close Encounters speaks to Utopianism, the belief within international relations theory that war can be eliminated either by perfecting man or by perfecting government (Cristol: 2011). Utopianism is also, of course, a key concept in science fiction. Raymond Williams includes amongst science fiction's utopian themes the 'willed transformation', in which a new kind of life is achieved by human effort, and 'technological transformation' in which a new ways of living are made possible by technical discovery (1979: 52). Both these themes can clearly be seen in *Close Encounters*; this, as a number of critics have noted, places Spielberg's film alongside the works of Jules Verne, Ray Bradbury and H.G. Wells as utopian science fiction.

Commenting on the transformative or transcendent in *Close Encounters*, Charlene Engel writes that the film 'suggests that humankind has reached the point where it is ready to enter the community of the cosmos.' (2002: 45-46). J.P. Telotte asserts that:

Close Encounters does hold out a key potential, a possibility for a combination of growth and renewal that might result from the alien/other experience and thus from the new sense of reality it brings. The film suggests that Neary and, by extension the rest of humanity, might grow to a new maturity, one... ultimately necessary for opening up to and understanding the human place in the universe.

[To this end] *Close Encounters* takes us to and beyond certain perceptual and epistemological limits, moves us into unfamiliar 'states'... if we can but go armed with this vision, we might, like Roy Neary, no longer feel quite so 'lost.' (2001: 151-160)

Close Encounters, in other words, is 'first contact read intentionally and transcendentally' (Cowan, 2010: 88). Or as Jack Kroll was the first to recognise in his *Newsweek* review back in 1977, 'in the rendezvous between earthlings and extraterrestrials you get the climax of Spielberg's optimism and his insistence that the best people are those who retain a childlike receptivity to the unknown' (1977: 92).

Synopsis

(*The following plot summary is based on the 1977* **Theatrical** *version; differences in the 1980* **Special Edition** *and 2001* **Collector's Edition** *(aka* **Director's Cut***) are discussed in Chapter 3.*)

Sonora Desert, Mexico – present day. Cartographer David Laughlin (Bob Balaban) becomes interpreter to Claude Lacombe (François Truffaut), both in a scientific team investigating the discovery in the desert of Flight 19: a squadron of bombers reported missing in 1945. No one seems to know how they got there, in perfect working order, and looking brand new. At an air traffic control centre in Indianapolis, two passenger jets report a near miss with an Unidentified Flying Object. That same night, four year old Barry Guiler (Cary Guffey) is woken when his battery operated toys suddenly come to life by themselves. He is drawn out of the farmhouse, waking his mother, Jillian (Melinda Dillon), who goes in search of him in the nearby woods.

Meanwhile, in the suburbs of Muncie, Indiana, power line repairman Roy Neary (Richard Dreyfuss) is called out to investigate a major blackout in the area. Finding himself lost on a country road, his truck is targeted by the blinding light of a mysterious craft that burns the skin on his face and causes his truck to temporarily lose power. Giving chase to the UFO, Roy almost runs down Barry at the moment Jillian finds him on the roadside. The three of them witness a number of UFOs fly past them. Returning home, Roy tries to convince his wife, Ronnie (Teri Garr) of what he saw, but Ronnie is sceptical and a little disturbed by her husband's claims, especially when Roy is fired from his job. The following night Roy goes back to the site of his encounter where he again meets Jillian and Barry amongst a gathering of people hoping for another sighting of the UFOs. They instead find themselves fleeing a fleet of government 'black helicopters' sent to disperse the crowd.

Lacombe and his team travel to India where villagers have heard 'music' emanating in the sky in the form of five musical tones endlessly repeated. Lacombe demonstrates how the five note sequence can be translated into visual communication by using Kodaly hand signals. The team repeatedly transmit the notes into space via satellite and receive back a sequence of numbers that Laughlin identifies as map co-ordinates of Wyoming.

Roy, meanwhile, has been having strange visions of a mountain shape, and feels compelled to sculpt it in clay in a bid to understand what it is. The UFOs descend upon Jillian's farmhouse; despite her attempts to barricade her home, Barry is abducted. At a meeting between UFO witnesses and military brass, Roy attempts to get answers. The army deny all knowledge of the UFOs; however, we see that an operation is underway to evacuate a stretch of Wyoming by the military and that a cover story is being planned to hide an impending event ('The Mayflower Project') involving Lacombe and his team.

Tormented by the strange mountain vision, and by his inability to understand what is happening to him, Roy begins to suffer a breakdown, and his family life falls apart. When Roy starts to build a giant version of the mountain inside the house, Ronnie takes the children and leaves. A television news flash reports on an area of Wyoming being evacuated due to the accidental release of nerve gas by the military: Roy discovers that the mountain shape is an actual place in Wyoming – a landmark called Devil's Tower.

Ignoring the warnings, Roy and Jillian travel to Wyoming but are captured by the army near Devil's Tower and taken to an evacuation centre, where Roy is interviewed by Lacombe and Laughlin. Recognising that Neary has been somehow 'chosen', Lacombe tries to make a case for him to remain, but his appeal is overturned by the military. Neary and Jillian manage to escape, and make a run to Devil's Tower.

As they climb the Tower, the army sends helicopters to release nerve gas. Roy and Jillian retreat into a box canyon where they discover a giant landing site that has been built for an arranged meeting between Lacombe's team and the UFOs. Roy and Jillian witness the landing of a giant Mothership, which communicates to Lacombe's team through the five musical tones. Abductees are released from the craft including the crew of Flight 19 and Barry, who is reunited with Jillian. Lacombe makes a special case for Roy to be included among a group of astronauts to board the Mothership. Extraterrestrials single Roy out from the rest of the astronauts, and he is invited to go with them. A lone extraterrestrial approaches Lacombe who attempts to communicate using the Kodaly hand signs. The extraterrestrial returns the greeting, before leaving in the Mothership with Roy on board.

Steven Spielberg on location with Close Encounters.

I. *Close Encounters*: Genre and Context

Early Sci-Fi

In the seventeen and eighteen hundreds the industrial revolution saw a response
in literature to the way science and technology was reshaping the world. Jules
Verne's stories of fantastic adventure, *From the Earth to the Moon* (1865), *Twenty
Thousand Leagues Under the Sea* (1870), *Around the World in 80 Days* (1873)
explored technological devices and transportation. H.G. Wells wrote cautionary tales
of scientific inventors – *The Island of Dr. Moreau* (1895), *The Invisible Man* (1897)
The Time Machine (1895) – and imagined Martian invasion in *The War of the Worlds*
(1897). In America, Edgar Rice Burroughs wrote of extraordinary realms in his *Martian
Adventures Series* (1912-1964), and of prehistoric reawakening in *The Land That Time
Forgot* (1918).

Science fiction exploded in the 1920s and 1930s, partly because of the popularity
of cinema, itself a wondrous time machine and magic show, but also thanks to pulp
magazines. The monthly *Amazing Stories* (1926) introduced writers like E.E. 'Doc'
Smith, and later Roger Zelazny and Ursula K. Le Guin, whilst *Astounding Science
Fiction* (1930), which would be later renamed *Analog* (and is still published today)
debuted Isaac Asimov, Theodore Sturgeon, A.E. Van Vogt and Robert Heinlein. Its
most famous editor was John W. Campbell Jr., author of *Who Goes There?* (1948) –
later adapted for the cinema as *The Thing From Another World* (1951) (Telotte, 2001:
63-122; Sobchack, 2001: 17-25).

After World War Two, pulp writers began publishing novels, helping to move science
fiction further into the mainstream. Key writers of this era include Ray Bradbury
(*Martian Chronicles* 1946-); Asimov (*I, Robot*, 1950, *The Foundation Trilogy*, 1951-);
Heinlein (*The Puppet Masters*, 1951) and Arthur C. Clark (*Childhood's End*, 1953).
The emergence of speculative fiction within 'serious' contemporary literature took
place at the same time, with the works of Aldous Huxley (*Brave New World*, 1931),
George Orwell *1984* (1948), and later J.G. Ballard (*The Drowned World*, 1962) and
Kurt Vonnegut (*Cat's Cradle*, (1963). These novels sought to combine fantasy with
philosophy and politics, drawing on allegory to comment on (often disturbing) trends

within modern society. Closely aligned are the traditions of utopian and dystopian literature. Utopian novels date back to Thomas More's *Utopia* (1516) and *Erehwon*, written in 1872 by Samuel Butler, which contrast idealised worlds with the failings of the present reality; dystopian works such as Bradbury's *Fahrenheit 451* (1953), on the other hand, depict a future characterised by oppressive social control and human misery (Sanders, 2009: 150-151; King and Krzywinska, 2000: esp. 13-22).

In cinema, Georges Méliès became the first sci-fi filmmaker of sorts. His *A Trip to the Moon* (1902) featured rocketships, interstellar travel and aliens. The age of modernity after World War One led to optimism about science and technology creating a better world, but also to fears about the inequalities of a technological society. Fritz Lang's *Metropolis* (1926) depicted a divided city where workers would become virtually enslaved by machines while the idle rich enjoyed the fruit of their labour. Class struggle in a futuristic (dystopic) environment has become a recurrent theme of science fiction cinema due to the lasting influence of *Metropolis* (*The Hunger Games*, 2012, *Snowpiercer*, 2013, *Mad Max: Fury Road*, 2015). By contrast, *Things to Come* (1936), adapted by H.G. Wells from his novel *The Shape of Things to Come* (1933) predicted a utopian future after war causes society to collapse and be replaced by a new improved one (Sanders, 2009: 140-154).

The film serials, *Flash Gordon* (1936) and *Buck Rogers* (1939) popularised pulp science fiction cinema in the form of rocketships, ray guns, alien invaders, evil intergalactic emperors and damsels in distress; and employed a machine-like narrative strategy of incessant cliff-hanger situations to hook the viewer into returning to the theatre each week. We can see them as the inspiration for the likes of *Star Wars* and the myriad superhero blockbuster movies that continue to dominate Hollywood today.

The bombings of Hiroshima and Nagasaki ushered in an atomic age which could be seen reflected in the radiation/alien-invasion fears of 1950s Cold War science fiction. *The Thing from Another World*, *The Day The Earth Stood Still*, *The War of the Worlds* (1953), *It Came from Outer Space*, *Invaders from Mars*, *Invasion of the Body Snatchers* (1956), clearly play on Cold War paranoia and the attendant national obsession in the late 1940s/ early 1950s with UFOs. Fears of radiation from atomic testing, radioactive fall-out or nuclear war found expression in films about atomic mutation and monster bugs: *Them!* (1954), *The Incredible Shrinking Man* (1957), *Tarantula* (1955) – the last two films directed by Jack Arnold, arguably sci-fi's first 'auteur' director. At the same time, space exploration films showed a more optimistic side of technology in the 1950s, as America and the-then U.S.S.R. competed in the 'space race': *Destination Moon* (1950), *Rocketship X-M* (1950), *When Worlds Collide* (1951), *Forbidden Planet* (1956) (Warren, 2010).

Aliens attack in Earth vs. The Flying Saucers *[1956].*

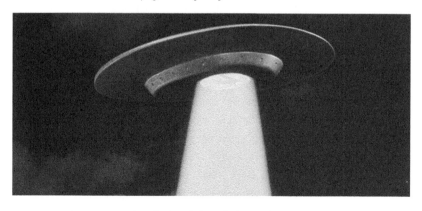

More saucer shenanigans in This Island Earth *[1955]. This one's beaming up a plane.*

Modern Sci-fi Cinema, 1968 onwards

In 1968, *2001: A Space Odyssey* returned science fiction to its origins in Greek mythology. Kubrick's landmark film can be seen as a culmination of the space exploration themes of the previous decade and one of the first to broach the need to evolve beyond imminent destruction at our own hands. As such it is perhaps the first example of 'transcendent' science fiction cinema, exploring the human need to place trust in a force larger than ourselves; given its lofty philosophical ambitions, however, its influence unsurprisingly took time to catch on in Hollywood mainstream terms (Cowan, 2010: esp. 3-71).

Science fiction films of the early seventies were instead more overtly concerned with identity and environment, and how both were increasingly shaped or misshapen by technology: *Silent Running* (1972) *Westworld* (1973), *Soylent Green* (1973), *The Omega Man* (1971) and *The Andromeda Strain* (1971). In low budget exploitation cinema, a number of notable creature features deliberately played on the public's fears of ecological imbalance and pollution: *Willard* (1971), *Frogs* (1972), *Night of the Lepus* (1972), *Killer Bees* (1974) and *Squirm* (1976).

Star Wars (1977) started as homage to the serials but its blockbuster status led to big-budget mythological science fiction a' la *2001*, making the genre bankable and relocating it from the cult to the mainstream with such box office hits as *Close Encounters, Alien* (1979) and *Star Trek: The Motion Picture* (1979). Then, in the 1980s, science fiction cinema entered its postmodern phase with *Blade Runner* (1982), *The Terminator* (1984) and *Robocop* (1987). In all of these narratives the robot/replicant/cyborg is prominent, raising questions about what it is to be 'human' in an age of Baudrillardian simulacra and simulation. Hybridity also came increasingly into play within the genre during this time. *Blade Runner*'s director, Ridley Scott, consciously drew on characteristics of film noir to create a 'tech-noir' hybrid in both narrative and visual design (Sobchack, 2001: 241-255). James Cameron combined science fiction and war movie in *Aliens* (1986). Indeed, *Close Encounters* originated as a mix of UFO movie and post-Watergate conspiracy thriller (as explored in Chapter 2) and contains elements of horror and domestic drama. (It can, and has, also been read as an example of 1970s New Hollywood Cinema and as an auteur work, all of which serve to enrich its meaning, as I hope to demonstrate in this book.)

Another sign of postmodernism in science fiction is the element of pastiche. In particular, the influence of other national cinemas impacted on the sci-fi films of the 1970s/80s. *Star Wars* famously adapted its plot from the Japanese film *Hidden Fortress* (1958) – indeed Kurosawa's films have also influenced such disparate titles as *Battle Beyond the Stars* (1980) (based on *The Seven Samurai*, 1954) and *Mad Max 2: The Road Warrior* (1981) (based on *Yojimbo*, 1961). Intertextuality is therefore a further key characteristic of 1970s/1980s sci-fi cinema, and, it follows, of *Close Encounters* (again, see Chapter 2).

Post 9/11 has seen a move towards such intelligent science fiction as a bankable commodity within Hollywood: *Solaris* (2002), *Primer* (2004), *Children of Men* (2006) *Sunshine* (2007), *Moon* (2009), *Inception* (2010), *Looper* (2012), *Oblivion* (2013), *Gravity* (2013) and *Interstellar* (2014) show that the genre has perennial box office appeal and proving sci-fi as one of the most durable and adaptable Hollywood genres. (According to *The Encyclopedia of Science Fiction*, in 1971 sci-fi, horror and fantasy accounted for approximately five per cent of US box-office takings; by 1982 this figure had risen to approach 50 per cent, and in 2010 it was nearly 90 per cent – www.sf-encyclopedia.com).

Science Fiction Cinema and Special Visual Effects

Part of the genre's continuing appeal is, of course, the showcasing of state of the art cinema technology within the sci-fi narrative. Special effects technology has evolved in line with cinema's own development. In the early days of silent film, for example, Georges Méliès was the first to use stop-motion, model work, double exposure, miniatures and matte paintings in his fantasy films. Animator Willis O'Brien developed stop-motion and models for *The Lost World* (1925), and was instrumental in creating arguably the greatest fantasy film of 'classical Hollywood', *King Kong*, in 1933. Later, the legendary Ray Harryhausen would perfect the use of stop-frame animation in a number of 1950s/60s science fiction fantasies including *The Beast from 20,000 Fathoms* (1953), *The Seventh Voyage of Sinbad* (1958), *Jason and the Argonauts*

(1963) and *One Million Years B.C.* (1966) which combined live action and models, and employed sophisticated matte processes.

Special Effects Supervisor Douglas Trumbull and director Stanley Kubrick pioneered motion control (computer controlled camera) in *2001: A Space Odyssey*, which, combined with painstaking model work of the spacecraft, created a new sense of realism in sci-fi films. John Dykstra (Trumbull's assistant on *2001*) used and improved upon many of those techniques in *Star Wars*, as did Trumbull in *Close Encounters*, utilising computer controlled models as well as a motion control camera to combine live actors, camera movements and special effects. In *Close Encounters*, Trumbull shot the special effects in 65mm to prevent degradation of the image. He employed front projection processes in several scenes and motion control so that camera movements could be incorporated into special effects shots. Over 100 shots involved matte paintings. Night photography and the glow of the UFOs created special challenges, which forced Trumbull and his Special Effects crew to find new solutions, making *Close Encounters* a landmark alongside *Star Wars* and *2001* in pre-CGI visual effects (Morton, 2007: 209-252; Turnock, 2015: 103-179). Animatronics, such as those utilised in *Close Encounters* to create the extraterrestrial, 'Puck', have featured in films since *Mary Poppins* (1964), Disney being a pioneer. Italian special effects artist Carlo Rambaldi brought animatronics to modern sci-fi cinema with *Close Encounters*, *ET*, *Alien* (1979), *Possession* (1981), and *Dune* (1984).

Photochemical effects such as those developed by Trumbull in *Close Encounters* have now, of course, been replaced by Computer Generated Imagery (although Trumbull returned to photochemical effects in 2011 for Terrence Malick's *The Tree of Life*). Director James Cameron was one of the pioneers of CGI in *The Abyss* (1989) which incorporated the technique of 'morphing', blending one image into the next. CGI was employed to nightmarish effect in *Terminator 2: Judgement Day* (1991) in which the liquid metal T1000 changes shape at will to mimic any object or person. Spielberg first experimented with CGI in the early stages of planning *Close Encounters*, but the power of computers back then was insufficient to render effects with anything like the level of realism needed. *Jurassic Park* (1993) became a landmark of CGI, creating dinosaurs and other prehistoric creatures that looked believable on the big screen, animated with a smoothness almost impossible to achieve with traditional stop-frame techniques. CGI could also blend live action and special effects seamlessly, without the use of mattes or multiple exposures. Accordingly, CGI has quickly dominated science fiction, taking the place of models, sets and matte paintings. *Avatar* (2009), *Inception* (2010) and *Tron: Legacy* (2010), in particular demonstrate the seemingly limitless possibilities that CGI offers in creating fantasy worlds. In terms of visual effects production *Industrial Light and Magic* have become the 'go-to' effects house with credits that include the *Jurassic Park*, *Harry Potter* and *Star Trek* franchises. In 2012 ILM was bought by *The Walt Disney Company* as part of its acquisition of Lucasfilm Ltd. Spielberg has worked with them on *AI: Artificial Intelligence* (2001), *Minority Report* (2002) and *War of the Worlds* (2005). Although *Close Encounters* now looks dated in some of its effects scenes, it holds up remarkably well, a testament to the time, patience and money spent on the visual effects.

2. *Close Encounters*: Influences and Production Background

The divided opinion of critics as outlined in my introduction in many ways reflects Spielberg's own ambivalence towards *Close Encounters*. Speaking in 2008 Spielberg commented, 'for me, *Close Encounters* was a work in progress and even now I feel it's a work in progress' (Bouzereau, 2008). That work in progress has included three versions of the film (The original *Theatrical Cut* released in cinemas in 1977; the re-edited *Special Edition* re-release in 1980; and the *Definitive Director's Version* given a limited theatrical release in the U.S. in 1998, and released as *The Collector's Edition* on DVD in 2001). No other Spielberg film has been subject to so much revision by its director (*E.T.* was re-released in a slightly extended version with minor CGI modifications in 2002). Of all his films, what compels Spielberg to keep returning to *Close Encounters*?

In 1997 Spielberg spoke from the set of *Saving Private Ryan* (1998) for the DVD documentary *The Making of Close Encounters*:

Twenty years later I look at my movie and I see a lot of naivety and I see my youth and I see my blind optimism, and I see how I've changed... I see how a little less optimistic (I am) the older I get... So I look at *Close Encounters* and I see a very sweet idealistic odyssey about a man who gives up everything in pursuit of his dream or his obsession. In 1997 I would never have made *Close Encounters* the way I made it in 1977 because I have a family that I would never leave. I would never drive my family out of house and home and build a papier mache mountain in the den, and then further leave them to get on a spaceship possibly never to return to them. I mean, that was just the privileges of youth. And when I see *Close Encounters* it's the one film I see that dates me, that I really look back and see who I was twenty years ago compared to who I am now. (Bouzereau, 1997)

However, ten years after making those comments, Spielberg seemed to have regained some of that youthful idealism at the heart of *Close Encounters* as he discussed in the DVD documentary *30 Years of Close Encounters* what he describes as his 'master image' in the film:

The image I've always taken sort of in bed with me at night if I ever flash on an image from *Close Encounters*, ...is when the little boy opens the door. And all that orange light, yellow light pours across him. When I designed the shot and when I wrote it in the script, for me it was very symbolic of what only a child can do, which is to trust the light, open the door; when an adult would run and hide and say 'Don't open the door, lock the door, there are things outside which we don't understand which could kill us or change us'. But the optimism of childhood in opening that door and light being the presence of everything... that light is something that boy wanted to know more about. And so for me, thematically, *Close Encounters* is all about children opening doors onto beautiful sources of light. 2007, twenty-first century, sadly people have a different interpretation of opening the doors, but back in the seventies to open the door to a curiosity was a safe experience and something we all looked forward to in our lives. (Bouzereau, 2008)

In his study of Spielberg, *Empire of Dreams*, Andrew M. Gordon identifies a conflict in Spielberg's characters 'between the rational adult self and the irrational child' (2008: 271) and how this plays out Spielberg's own conflicts about growing into mature adulthood, marriage and fatherhood. Most of Spielberg's later films, as Gordon points out, are 'conversion narratives about reluctant fathers or father figures forced through adversity to recognize their responsibility to their children' (ibid.) And yet in these films (*Jurassic Park* [1993], and *War of the Worlds* [2005] most notably) that conversion narrative is awkwardly grafted on to the sci-fi/ fantasy premises of the films, suggesting that this conflict remains essentially unresolved. Many critics have suggested that this conflict may have resulted from Spielberg's own childhood; to the divorce of his parents when he was still in his teens.

However, the child/adult dichotomy is not the only conflict at play in *Close Encounters*. In his 1986 essay *Blissing Out*, the critic Andrew Britton discussed what he sees as a further ambivalence in Spielberg, ideologically, in terms of his sincerity as an artist on the one hand and his cynicism as a maker of 'popcorn' entertainment on the other. These two drives might, in fact, not so much conflict as for the most part coalesce:

It is the essence of Spielberg's case that the cynicism and the sincerity consort quite naturally with each other – that they become, that is, a third thing which is neither simply the one nor simply the other. (2009: 141)

The consorting cynicism and sincerity is further complicated by certain other related conflicts in Spielberg: in his desire to break box office records whilst at the same time stamp his films with an auteur trademark; in his attempts to combine (often in the same film) blockbuster narrative with personal artistic expression, creative independence with movie mogul-ism. These conflicts are what often result, in Spielberg's films, in the 'blips': the lapses into sentimentality, the weakened compromised endings. The cynicism and sincerity may not always consort quite so naturally in all of his work. Part of why Spielberg returned to *Close Encounters* in 1980 was because he felt that 'certain compromises had to be made as a result of budget and schedule' (McBride, 1997: 290). He did not feel his vision was fully realised. But his return to the film again in 1997 was in order to correct the mistakes of the *Special Edition*, itself the result of compromises made for the studio, Columbia Pictures, who requested he added a scene near the end of the film which took us inside the Mothership.

In his study of Spielberg for *Senses of Cinema*, Stephen Rowley astutely comments that *Close Encounters* is 'an ambitious but uneven work, too scruffy to be the unqualified masterpiece Spielberg wanted it to be...it is a curious blend: a domestic drama; a thriller about a government cover-up; a light horror film with a creepy science-fiction menace; and a globe-trotting, quasi-epic portrayal of the first contact between human and alien...a reminder that flawed films can be more rewarding than films that are perfectly executed but less ambitious' (2006).

'A flawed movie but a great movie,' John Landis remarks on *Trailers from Hell*. 'It has all the *good* things about Steven Spielberg, and *some* of the bad.'

And so *Close Encounters* remains a work in progress, an on-going solution: sincere despite its cynicism, heartfelt despite its popcorn populism, childlike *and* childish.

Close Encounters: **Influences and Intertextuality**

Critics have noted a number of filmic influences on *Close Encounters*, which give it an element of intertextuality and sometimes 'act as subliminal commentary on the action' (Gordon, 2008: 57). In his compendium on Spielberg's films, Ian Freer, for example, lists 1950s science fiction movies, *2001: A Space Odyssey*, Walt Disney, John Ford's *The Searchers* (1956), Hitchcock and Frank Capra amongst the eclectic references to movie history woven into the fabric of *Close Encounters* (2001: 63-64.) Rather than lending *Close Encounters* an air of postmodern pastiche (cf. *Independence Day* [1996]), however, the intertextuality of *Close Encounters* helps to shape its inner meaning and philosophy.

Richard Carlson confronts shady alien visitors in It Came From Outer Space.

Already noted is the 'benevolent view of alien visitors... traceable to flicks such as *The Day the Earth Stood Still* and *It Came from Outer Space*' (ibid.) In both films, aliens are seen as 'saviours', as Paul Buhle and Dave Wagner point out, warning governments on earth of the dangers of the nuclear arms race, and advocating peaceful co-existence between East and West. The aliens are portrayed in each as superior beings leading humankind 'into a new age of goodwill' (2005: 75-76). Ray Bradbury wrote the original story on which *It Came...* was based, and his influence on Spielberg's vision is evident. Joseph McBride observes that Spielberg responded in his youth to the 'poetic nature of Bradbury's work, its way of magically transforming reality'; and that Spielberg once remarked to Bradbury himself that *Close Encounters* 'wouldn't have been born if I hadn't seen *It Came*… six times when I was a kid' (McBride, 1997: 121). Bradbury, for his part, recognised a kinship between his work and Spielberg's, praising *Close Encounters* repeatedly over the years. In his review for the L.A Times in 1977, Bradbury went as far as describing *Close Encounters* as 'the most important film of our time', and claimed to prefer it to *2001*, writing '*Close Encounters* knows exactly where the center of the universe is' (Freer, 2001: 72).

Kubrick's film is, however, a major influence on Spielberg's in a number of ways.

2001: A Space Odyssey

Of seeing *2001* for the first time as a film student, Spielberg recalled to documentary maker Paul Joyce in a TV tribute to Stanley Kubrick filmed in 1999:

> The first time I saw *2001* was in Hollywood at the Pantages Theater, and I was a student at Cal State, Long Beach. … And of course the entire campus was talking about *2001*. They were talking about the fact that it was a drug movie. Now that was kind of strange for me because I never took any drugs…But I came out of the end of that picture much higher than any of my friends who had taken mind altering substances. …Since *2001* no documentary, no other movie, no IMAX experience being on the shuttle looking down at earth, has ever put me in space as much as *2001* did. It made me fear it and made me want it so desperately; want to be part of that great mystery; want to be at the forefront of the pioneers that would discover the monolith, the stargate and what lies beyond.

2001 informs *Close Encounters* in theme and plot. The origins of evolution, its possible links to extraterrestrial intelligence, and mankind's search for his place in the universe, are philosophic themes central to both films. Like *2001*, *Close Encounters* is, at its core, concerned with our journey to the sublime, towards a state of higher consciousness. But Spielberg's vision hinges not so much on cool scientific intellect being the key to our next stage of evolution, as on the necessary development of *emotional* intelligence: to that end we must regain our childlike curiosity for what lies beyond, we must recover our capacity to experience wonder at the mysteries of the universe.

In *2001*, it is not so much a condition of dehumanisation (as critics tend to describe it) as a state of remarkable technological complacency that makes humankind so in need of transcendent evolution through alien contact (the same technological complacency which leads to doomsday in *Dr Strangelove* [1965]). Journeying to Clavius in *2001*, Floyd and his fellow astronauts are just as excited – if not more so – by their synthetic chicken and ham sandwiches as they are by the prospect of encountering extraterrestrial intelligence. Complacency in *2001* leads to the creation of Hal 9000, the computer supposedly free from human malfunction, which proves to be mankind's ultimate failed experiment, his grand folly. In *Close Encounters* complacency takes the form of the comfortable but vapid suburban existence from which Roy must finally emerge if he is to achieve self-actualisation. Both films share as their master image the 'star child', a symbol of rebirth into the cosmos; in Kubrick's film the star child is literalised in *2001*'s final moments as an infant foetus; in Spielberg's film, as Bradbury points out, 'we are... the star-children' (Freer, 2001: 72), like Roy and little Barry, Lacombe and the other UFO contactees, drawn to the 'threshold of beyond'.

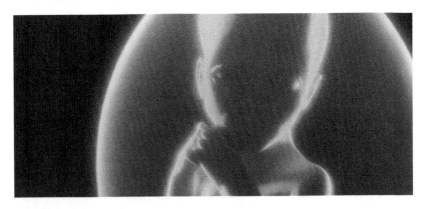

The Star Child of 2001: A Space Odyssey.

The use of a cover story by government and military in *Close Encounters* to ensure that first contact remains a secret is a plot device borrowed from *2001*. In Kubrick's film rumour of an epidemic on the Clavius moonbase is circulated to conceal the discovery of the alien sentinel monolith. In *Close Encounters*, the military, aided by the national media, use the cover story of a nerve gas spillage in order to clear the Devil's Tower area of civilian witnesses to the impending UFO landing. 'I'm sure that you're all aware of the extremely grave potential for cultural shock and social disorientation contained in this present situation if the facts were prematurely and suddenly made public without adequate preparation and conditioning', Dr Floyd advises his fellow scientists in *2001*. In *Close Encounters*, the government is shown similarly trying to 'insulate us from any disturbing and thus potentially dangerous revelations' (Telotte, 2001: 152). Moreover, Spielberg develops what is a minor plot point in *2001* into a major subplot in Close Encounters which is both a philosophical commentary on the government's role as, in Telotte's words, 'a kind of protective parent…doing all it can to keep the people in a preternaturally childish state' (ibid.) and a direct reference to the UFO cover up theories of the 1970s, by way of the post-Watergate Hollywood conspiracy thriller subgenre popularised by such films as *The Parallax View* (1974) and *All the President's Men* (1976). Indeed, *Close Encounters* started off as a story in the vein of 'UFOs and Watergate', as I discuss later.

Government cover ups have figured in sci-fi films before and after *2001* and *Close Encounters*, however, reflecting on-going cultural anxieties. Several years before *Close Encounters*, the made-for-television movie *The Disappearance of Flight 412* (1974) featured a mysterious government agency that detains and indoctrinates an air force crew after they report a UFO on a flying mission in the American southwest. More recently with the advent of the internet, conspiracy theories have proliferated and Hollywood has responded with a number of films and TV series about UFO and government cover-ups. *The X-Files* television series (1993-2002; 2015-) and feature film spin offs (1998, 2008) included a major story arc that saw FBI agents uncover a government conspiracy to hide the existence of aliens on earth. NBC's short-lived *Dark Skies* (1996-1997) presented a similar cover up, in which aliens are revealed to have been among humans since the 1940s but their presence concealed by the government. UFO/alien abduction conspiracies also feature in the TV show *Roswell* [aka *Roswell High*](1999-2002), *Fire in the Sky* (1993), the Spielberg executive-produced TV miniseries *Taken* (2002), *The Forgotten* (2004), *Ejecta* (2014), *The Rendlesham UFO Incident* [aka *Hanger 10*] (2014) and the comedy spoofs *Alien Autopsy* (2006) and *Paul* (2011).

In some ways, though, perhaps the greatest influence of *2001* on *Close Encounters* arises from the Kubrickian view of the 'God Concept'. Interviewed by *Playboy* magazine after the release of *2001* in 1968, Kubrick commented on the religious interpretations placed on his film:

> [T]he God concept is at the heart of *2001* but not any traditional, anthropomorphic image of God. I don't believe in any of Earth's monotheistic religions, but I do believe that one can construct an intriguing *scientific* definition of God once you accept (the possibility of superintelligent extraterrestrial lifeforms) whose potentialities would be limitless and their intelligence ungraspable by humans... these beings would *be* gods to the billions of less advanced races in the universe...they would possess the twin attributes of all deities – omniscience and omnipotence. They would be incomprehensible to us except as gods; and if the tendrils of their consciousness ever brushed men's minds, it is only the hand of God we could grasp as an explanation. (Nordern, 1968: 49-50 original emphases)

In *Close Encounters*, the extraterrestrials are portrayed in similar terms, as superintelligent beings, although their relationship to human civilisation differs to Kubrick's vision of an extraterrestrial entity of pure energy and spirit guiding and ultimately *controlling* the evolution of mankind. Spielberg's aliens are more like extraterrestrial good neighbours than gods, lending friendly support and assistance during our time of existential need.

Disney

Andrew Gordon, conversely, describes *Close Encounters* as a 'purified, Disneyized version of religion' (1980: 156), and it is true that the influence of Disney on *Close Encounters* (and Spielberg generally) has been commented on by a number of critics, often pejoratively. Spielberg has frequently been compared to Disney, primarily for the manner in which 'many of his films either evoke childhood or convey a childlike sense of wonder' (Kendrick, 2014: 6). Spielberg's exposure to Disney as a child was primarily through the medium of television and, according to Frederick Wasser, Disney's influence on viewers of Spielberg's age through the TV shows was a 'more conservative force than the other Hollywood movies starting to appear on television (in the 1950s)' (2013: 21). Steven Watts contends that Disney's anti-Communist Cold War ideology during those years promulgated an inward-looking notion 'that the nuclear family with its attendant rituals of marriage, parenthood, emotional and spiritual instruction, and consumption, was the centerpiece of the American way of life...a bulwark in America's defense against enemies both foreign and domestic' (2013: 326).

Whilst Spielberg may appear to conform to the 'Disney Doctrine' in many ways, his willingness also to represent the dystopia of contemporary American life in *Close Encounters* marks a significant divergence. As Wasser notes, 'unlike the postwar Disney, Spielberg's writers were not burdened by a need to celebrate in the face of communist threat. Indeed, if they had painted too much of a white-picket-fence picture of Americana, they would certainly have given up the "hip" aspect of the contemporary blockbuster code' (2013: 73).

However, in *Close Encounters* Spielberg makes specific textual references to the Disney films, *Pinocchio* and *Fantasia* (both 1940). Introducing us to Roy Neary in *Close Encounters*, a close up of a child's music box in the shape of Pinocchio plays a rendition of 'When You Wish Upon a Star'. This song from the Disney film had been one of Spielberg's inspirations for *Close Encounters*, evoking in him a sense of wonder at the mysteries of the stars and the cosmos (as will be discussed in greater detail later in the chapter). In this context, the puppet boy Pinocchio's longing to become 'real' is clearly analogous to Roy's quest for transcendence. Spielberg would return to the Pinocchio story again to similar bitter-sweet effect in *AI: Artificial Intelligence* (2001), the story of a robot child who wants to become a real boy. In both films the yearning for a seemingly impossible transformation adds poignancy to the narrative. Boarding the Mothership at the end of *Close Encounters*, Roy, in Spielberg's words, 'becomes a real person. He loses his strings, his wooden joints, and...he makes the most important decision in the history of the world' (McBride, 1997: 283).

Similarly, in the final landing of the Mothership at Devil's Tower, Spielberg references the 'Night on Bald Mountain' sequence in *Fantasia*, with its giant shadow-casting spaceship evocative both of the demon lord Chernabog sweeping down over the mountain to envelope the town below and of Mother Night, 'blocking out the stars and clouds and pulling a veil of muddy darkness over everything' (Sragow, 1982: 115).

The Searchers

As well as Disney and the science fiction directors of the 1950s, critics have detected elements of other great American filmmakers in *Close Encounters*. Writing in *New York Magazine* in 1979, Stuart Byron includes *Close Encounters* amongst a group of films in the New Hollywood which seemed to have been markedly influenced by John Ford's classic western, *The Searchers* (1956). 'Sometimes the directors deny the influence,' wrote Byron, 'and often the influence is structural rather than direct, but in one way or another *The Searchers* relates (to)...*Taxi Driver* (1976), *Close Encounters*, *Hardcore* (1979) and *The Deerhunter* (1978): in each, 'an obsessed man searches for someone – a woman, a child, a best friend – who has fallen into the clutches of an alien people. But when found, the sought one doesn't want to be rescued.' In the case of *Close Encounters*, Byron argues that the Fordian influence can be seen in the obsessive search for Barry Guiler who has been abducted by the extraterrestrials (1979: 45-48).

When interviewed by Byron, Spielberg told him, '*The Searchers* has so many superlatives going for it. It's John Wayne's best performance to date. It's a study in dramatic framing and composition. It contains the single most harrowing moment in any film I've ever seen. It is high on my twenty five-favourite films list' (ibid., 46). However, he denied that he had been consciously influenced by *The Searchers*. It is true that Spielberg had, at the time of the interview, seen *The Searchers* 'a dozen times' (and has continued to watch it several times since) including twice on location for *Close Encounters*. But then Spielberg screened a number of films during the filming of *Close Encounters* and apparently took inspiration from many of them (Morton, 2007: 178; Balaban, 1978: 107).

Having said this, there are some striking similarities between the two films beside the basic plot. Both include sequences which depict the homestead under siege: in *The Searchers* a family barricades its home against attack by the Comanche; in *Close Encounters*, Jillian similarly attempts to shutter up her house against alien invaders who have come to abduct her child; and certain lighting effects, shots and aspects of mise-en-scène in *Close Encounters* (including the famous image of Barry opening the door to the ominous orange light) are comparable to those of Ford's film.

Hitchcock and Capra

The 'abduction of Barry' scene in *Close Encounters* also owes a significant debt to the home invasion sequences of *The Birds* (1963). Generally, Spielberg's 'dexterity with suspense and thrills has been likened to Alfred Hitchcock' (Kendrick, 2014: 6), a comparison already being made by critics at the time of *Close Encounters* on the basis of Spielberg's previous films, *Duel* (1971) and *Jaws* (1975). Spielberg's manipulation of suspense in the scene represents a temporary tonal shift to 'light horror… with a creepy science-fiction menace' (Rowley, 2006). The remote setting further evokes the isolated farmhouse under attack in *The Birds*. Christopher Sharrett has commented that in Hitchcock's film 'the belief in the recuperability of society begins to disappear….(there is) recognisable disintegration within the human community' (2002: 358). Kendrick has observed accordingly that in *Close Encounters* characters are subject to 'physical, spiritual and psychological invasion' and that 'to exorcise his fixation, Roy must destroy his suburban existence' (2014: 51-53). Like the humans in *The Birds*, Roy is shocked out of his sterile complacency by a potentially apocalyptic series of events.

The adventure thrillers of Hitchcock are also an influence on *Close Encounters*, particularly *North by Northwest*, whose last scene on Mount Rushmore is quoted in the sequence in which Roy and Jillian clamber up the Devil's Tower. In Hitchcock's film the woman slips and is saved by the man. Spielberg, as Warren Buckland has noted, reverses the gender roles of Hitchcock's film, 'for it is Roy who needs saving, not Jillian' (2006: 127), thereby increasing the suspense in the sequence – and the irony – as it is the main protagonist who is at risk. Central to both Hitchcock's and

CONSTELLATIONS

Spielberg's cinema is audience identification – we are invited through subjective shots and camera movement to be the characters. And typically in Spielberg's films as in Hitchcock's, the ordinary man is placed in extraordinary circumstances.

This preoccupation with the ordinary man has also prompted critics to compare Spielberg to Frank Capra. James Kendrick reflects that this comparison is generally based on 'the emotional effectiveness and general popularity of his (Spielberg's) films, as well as the recurring figure of the flawed but admirable everyman' (2014: 6). Spielberg has compared himself to Capra: 'my central protagonist has always been – and probably always will be – Mr. Everyday Regular Fella...each of my movies has showed enough humanity to allow the audience to identify with the person who is having the experience. I haven't made my *It's a Wonderful Life*. I haven't done that yet. I will someday' (Tuchman, 1978: 43-50). However, Andrew Britton, writing in 1986, contends that by pitting his everyman against forces of antagonism that are fantastical and purely escapist in nature (trucks; sharks, UFOs), Spielberg wilfully 'misreads Capra' (1986: 139).

Arguably, Spielberg wouldn't undertake to explore the corruption of the real world (explicitly at least) until his later films – *The Color Purple* (1985), *Empire of the Sun* (1987), *Schindler's List* (1993), *Saving Private Ryan* (1998), *Munich* (2005), *War Horse* (2011), *Lincoln* (2012), *Bridge of Spies* (2015) – which pit his everyman characters against true life social evils. In *Close Encounters* there *is*, however, an undeniable humanity that invites identification with the characters, and throughout *Close Encounters* Spielberg emphasises the impact of the alien visitation on the lives of normal everyday folk, and by extension mankind as a whole.

Although, as we have seen, *Close Encounters* is indeed 'crammed full of references to movie history' (Freer, 2001: 61), Spielberg's primary influence on *Close Encounters* arguably was not a film or a fictional source, but a serious scientific enquiry into the UFO phenomenon, written in 1972 by Dr J. Allen Hynek.

The UFO Experience

J. Allen Hynek was an astrophysicist and consultant for US Air Force's Project Blue

Dr. J Allen Hynek.

Book, the official investigator of UFO reports in the United States from 1947 to 1969. During this time, Hynek interrogated many hundreds of people and personally investigated as many cases, focussing on the experiences of the witnesses as well as the phenomena they claimed to observe. At first sceptical of the UFO phenomenon, Hynek came to find that the majority of eyewitnesses were credible individuals – police officers, pilots, air traffic controllers and the like – and that a significant number of UFO sightings could not be explained by natural phenomena.

Project Blue Book (originally Project Sign) was set up at the Wright–Patterson Air Force Base in Dayton, Ohio in September 1947, following a series of public UFO sightings that had started with pilot Kenneth Arnold's famous sighting near Mount Rainer, Washington on June 24, that year. Project Sign's purpose, at first, was to investigate these UFO sightings, and to try to determine the nature of the Unidentified Flying Objects that were being reported. However, when this initial wave of UFO sightings continued into 1948 and then 1949, the Pentagon began to subtly ridicule the phenomenon rather than investigate it seriously; Project Sign became Project Blue Book in the summer of 1951, whose unstated purpose became to debunk all UFO reports no matter how credible. Hynek found himself increasingly at odds with Air Force officials, who eventually dismissed further investigations following a report by University of Colorado scientists which concluded, according to the *Schenectady Gazette* (January 10, 1969), that there was 'no direct evidence whatever of a convincing nature' to support the existence of UFOs. Project Blue Book was subsequently closed in December 1969.

Hynek, however, was certain that not all UFO reports were hoaxes or misperceptions, and continued to receive UFO sighting reports through his office at Northwestern University, later setting up the *Center for UFO Studies* (which still operates today) dedicated to continuing the examination and analysis of the UFO phenomenon. In 1972 Hynek wrote *The UFO Experience: A Scientific Report*, drawing together reports from his years at Project Blue Book, 'an attempt to portray the kinds of things that people – real everyday human beings with jobs and families – say they have actually experienced' (Hynek, 1972: 8).

Spielberg's title for the film famously stems from J. Allen Hynek's categorisation of different types of UFO experience. Hynek classified reports into two main divisions: (i) those reports where a UFO has been observed at distance; (ii) those involving close-range sightings. The first category of reported sightings included lights seen in the night sky (Nocturnal Lights); oval or disc shaped objects seen in the daytime (Daylight Discs); and Unidentified Flying Objects observed by radar (Radar-Visual). Hynek divided the second category involving close-range sightings into three further subdivisions:

Close Encounters of the First Kind: in which the reported UFO is seen at close range but there is no interaction with the environment (other than trauma on the part of the observer);

Close Encounters of the Second Kind: similar to the First Kind, but there is physical evidence of the UFO (most notably flattened, scorched or broken trees and vegetation; cars and other vehicles temporarily losing power to their engines, headlights and radios during the encounter);

Close Encounters of the Third Kind: in which the presence of 'occupants' in or about the UFO is reported. (ibid., 44-47)

However, Spielberg's debt to *The UFO Experience* extends beyond his appropriation of Hynek's classification terms: many of the events in Spielberg's film are based on the eyewitness reports included in Hynek's book. This lends *Close Encounters* an air of authenticity in certain scenes, particularly the early sequences depicting an Air Traffic control sighting and Roy's initial encounter on the desolate Indiana highway. Indeed the Air Traffic control scene closely follows testimonies of radar-visual observers in Hynek's book. In one particular report, the pilot of a passenger jet describes an object with flashing coloured lights moving with terrific acceleration. The air traffic controller's radar 'paints' an Unidentified Flying Object on the screen, and he warns the pilot that the object is getting closer. The UFO then seems to play a game of cat and mouse with the jet before taking off at a vertical angle. The report, just like in the film, ends with the pilot being asked 'do you want to report a UFO?' and the pilot's response, again as in the film, is simply, 'No. We don't want to report' (ibid., 96-99).

Similarly, Roy's close encounter on the highway plays out as an amalgamation of similar encounters reported in *The UFO Experience*. Hynek writes that in a typical Close Encounter of the Second Kind (such as the one Roy experiences in the film), 'cars are seemingly always accosted on lonely roads' (ibid., 151) and that observers have reported physical effects such as 'temporary paralysis, numbness, a feeling of heat and other discomfort. "Interference" with the local gravitational field (results in) temporary feelings of weightlessness...car engines cease functioning' (ibid., 144-145). In the film, Roy's truck is suddenly enveloped by a blinding white light from above. The engine and radio in his truck go dead. Roy's skin is burned when he attempts to look out of the window at the source of the light. He becomes almost weightless inside the truck as gravity is lost. Then the encounter abruptly ends as the UFO moves away and Roy sees the same 'searchlight' from the UFO appear further down the highway. In *The UFO Experience* Hynek includes reports of strikingly similar phenomena given by various different witnesses but one particular close encounter experienced by a schoolteacher on a lonely road outside a small town in Wisconsin at night offers almost a prototype for Roy's experience in the film:

My engine, lights and radio went out and stopped...when I looked out of my windowshield... there it was above us...It was like an Indian sunset or something in color...I tried to start the car and I tried and tried, and as long as that thing was above us I just couldn't get that car to go...It was an eerie quiet...Another thing I remember...as though I was light in weight and airy...It felt like the air and everything was light and weightless...My feet were burning...it felt like scalding dry heat on them...Finally when it left the car...I saw it crossing the railway tracks, and it was going slowly down [the tracks]. (ibid., 152-153)

Other incidents in *The UFO Experience* seem to have inspired Spielberg. A high speed chase between the police and a UFO is described in the book, where 'for more than 70 miles the object was chased, at speeds sometimes as high as 105 miles per hour' (ibid., 133). Moreover, Spielberg clearly noted as he read *The UFO Experience* the adverse effects – psychological and emotional – that these close encounters had on the witnesses that Hynek interviewed. The police officer involved in the high speed pursuit of the UFO was, according to Hynek, 'singled out for unbearable ridicule and the pressure of unfavourable publicity. The combination of events wrecked his home life, estranged him from his wife, and ruined his career and health.' Hynek also tells of witnesses who suffered 'physiological and psychological after-effects...disturbed dreams...even changed life outlook and philosophy stemming from the encounter. To a few it has been akin to a religious experience' (ibid., 150). Like Roy in the film, many witnesses, Hynek wrote, 'wanted an explanation that would comfortably fit into their world picture so that they could be relieved of the burden of the frightening unknown' (ibid., 31).

More than just the reports from people who experienced close encounters, then, Spielberg also adopted Hynek's approach to the subject matter, his 'attempt to portray the kinds of things that people – real everyday human beings with jobs and families – say they have actually experienced'. Although Spielberg claims to be a UFO agnostic, he recognised in 1972 a growing cultural phenomenon that was not remote but taking place 'right in the heart of American suburbia' (Combs, 1977: 31).

When Spielberg read *The UFO Experience* it, in fact, rekindled a long term personal interest in the UFO phenomenon that had begun as a teenager growing up in Arizona, and which had already resulted in Spielberg's feature length amateur film, *Firelight*, made in 1964 when he was sixteen. Little wonder, then, that Spielberg considers *Close Encounters* a 'continuous work in progress': this early 8mm prototype also concerns the twin sci-fi staples of UFOs and alien abduction.

Firelight (1964)

Spielberg's two hour- twenty minute amateur film grew from a childhood obsession with science fiction literature, especially the work of Bradbury, H.G. Wells, Arthur C. Clarke and Robert Heinlein. Spielberg's biographer Joseph McBride suggests that Clarke's novel *Childhood's End* may have had a particular influence on the young filmmaker (1997: 105). Spielberg himself has described *Firelight* as 'more of an exploratory movie along the lines of *The Creeping Unknown* (1955) [U.K. *The Quatermass Experiment*]' (Spielberg, in Crawley, 1983: 29).

Firelight focusses on the attempts of two scientists to prove that extraterrestrials are abducting inhabitants in a small Arizona town. The scientists discover that the aliens, called Alterians, are transporting abductees to an interplanetary zoo, where they are reprogrammed in order to eradicate their human tendencies towards violence and hatred in a bid to prevent the imminent destruction of the Earth. As McBride notes, *Firelight* 'derives in large part from the mood of anxiety and paranoia' that characterised 1950s science fiction and may have reflected Spielberg's own fears of nuclear Armageddon during the Cold War (1997: 105). As in *Childhood's End* and *The Day the Earth Stood Still* (another clear influence on *Firelight*), the extraterrestrials act as an interstellar peace keeping force, who intervene to prevent man's extinction. Spielberg also includes a domestic subplot in which one of the scientists becomes attracted to the other scientist's wife, a complication that may have been a coded expression of Spielberg's own problems in dealing with his parents' disintegrating marriage. As a forerunner to *Close Encounters*, *Firelight* introduces themes of 'supernatural intruders, suburban alienation and escape, broken families and abducted children, scientific adventure and spiritual renewal' (McBride, 1997: 105). Like *Close Encounters* it initially presents an ambiguous, even menacing, viewpoint of aliens, before revealing them as ultimately benign and acting for the greater good.

CONSTELLATIONS

For an amateur film, *Firelight* is ambitious in scope as well as length. Spielberg filmed in various locations around his hometown of Phoenix, Arizona: Sky Harbor Airport, Phoenix Baptist Hospital, the local National Guard armoury and in the desert near Camelback Mountain National Park (McBride, 1997: 104). He shot *Firelight* on a Bolex-H8 8mm camera, with a magnetic sound stripe added to the cut footage afterwards for post-syncing the music, sound effects and dialogue. Spielberg created the visual effects himself, using a 'wide range of effects, from miniatures to stop-motion animation to some simple opticals' (Morton, 2007: 24).

As *Starburst* magazine reported in 1983, much of *Firelight* is lost. The story goes that when trying to break into Hollywood in the late 1960s, Spielberg would show his amateur films – including *Firelight* – to anyone who took an interest. After he gave a reel or two of *Firelight* to a producer to screen at his leisure, Spielberg learned when he later returned to collect his film that the man had been fired. 'Gone! His office was cleared out and now there's a Toyota dealership where the office used to be...So part of *Firelight* still exists, but all the exposition is gone' (Crawley, 1983: 31).

Clips that survive of *Firelight* strongly evoke the UFO movies that Spielberg watched as a teenager. His young protagonists are straight-laced clean teens conservatively dressed in early 1960s fashions. Young lovers break off their gentle petting and gape at the sky as mysterious red lights (created by Spielberg placing red gel filters in front of a spotlight) hover above suburbia. The hero, Tony Karcher (Robert Robyn) and his wife, Debbie (Beth Weber) drive along a dark highway as the mysterious lights cross the Arizona mountain range. Spielberg shoots his car sequences 'poor man's process' (actually filmed in his father's garage, converted by the young filmmaker into a makeshift studio), rocking the stationary vehicle back and forth to create the illusion of movement. Cut to a shot through the wing mirror of the mysterious red lights in close pursuit. Pan to Tony's startled reaction in the same mirror. He floors the gas pedal. Then a drive-by shot, filmed night for night, near Phoenix. Later in the film, another couple, parked on lovers' lane. The girl sees something terrifying through the windscreen and cries out to her beau next to her. He looks up and Spielberg crash zooms into his awestruck face. Cut to an impressive wide shot of their parked car on the desert highway, lit by moonlight; ahead of them, a giant glowing red light...

Despite its technical virtuosity, is *Firelight* recognisably a Spielberg film? Writing in *The New Yorker*, Richard Brody commented 'what is fascinating about Spielberg's early shorts is that they are utterly derivative of the pop culture that he had been consuming' (March, 5, 2012). Brody accurately describes those shorts as precocious, but made by someone who had done an impressive job of duplicating the work of a veteran TV director. Spielberg himself, on being asked if his early amateur films are recognisably his, replied 'they're recognisably home movies with youngsters in cowboy hats and German combat helmets' (Tuchman, 1978: 40). Indeed, the fragments of *Firelight* that remain, impressive though they are in their solid (stolid) professionalism, show that Spielberg did *not* necessarily display his now-trademark visual panache from an early age. Richard Zanuck, who co-produced *The Sugarland Express* and *Jaws*, describes Spielberg as having an 'innate sense of the visual mechanics of how you put all the pieces together so that that the result is very striking' (Morton, 2007: 36). Arguably, Spielberg is one of the cinema's great pictorialists, in the tradition of D.W. Griffith and Cecil B. DeMille, narrating story through a series of visually powerful tableaux. This ability he developed during his professional career; it is not especially apparent in those early shorts. Instead, *Firelight* and his earlier amateur films (*Fighter Squad* [1960; *Escape to Nowhere* [1962]), when compared to the French New Wave-inspired formal experimentation of, say, Martin Scorsese's early student shorts (*What's a Nice Girl Like You Doing in A Place Like This* [1962]; *It's Not Just You, Murray* [1964]) speak to Spielberg's provincial upbringing, a lack of cultural input beyond the television and mainstream films rationed out by his parents during those formative years. 'In Phoenix, Arizona, television never really carried very good movies...We didn't have a good art house where I could see a Preston Sturges retrospective or Frank Capra films... It wasn't until I was professionally making films that I began to see some of the old pictures and have my own renaissance in film appreciation.' (Tuchman, 1978: 39).

Firelight shows how Spielberg could easily have gone on to become a John Guillermin or a Joseph Sargent, the kind of 'hard-hatted journeyman', that he ultimately decided not to be after several years as a TV director, finding instead a place amongst the New Hollywood with Scorsese, Coppola, Altman and De Palma, doing 'something a little more personal' (ibid, 46). Brody aptly describes Spielberg's early cine club-type

A 16 year old Spielberg poses outside of The Phoenix Little Theatre on the day of his Firelight
premiere.

pastiches as 'the most impersonal sort of personal filmmaking. He was, in effect,
America's oldest young filmmaker' (*The New Yorker*, 2012).

There is, however, one signature Spielberg shot in *Firelight* that would become a
significant feature of *Close Encounters*. As the child abductee (played by Steven's
younger sister, Nancy) crawls across the grass to touch the mysterious red light that
has landed in her backyard, her mother screams and the camera tracks forward into
a close up of the woman's terrified face; the camera movement magnifying the
character's emotional state. This 'push in' camera would be used to powerful effect
throughout *Close Encounters*. As Ian Freer states, *Close Encounters* is 'dominated by
tracking (or dolly) shots, usually towards a character looking up in awe at something
bigger than life. A kind of visual shorthand for impending wonder' (2001: 66).

Close Encounters: Script Development

Although Spielberg would eventually structure *Close Encounters of the Third Kind* around an everyman character and how that person might respond to a close encounter with something he doesn't fully understand, it actually took Spielberg a long time to find his story. 'I had a lot of scenarios for hanging a UFO story on,' he revealed in 1997. 'One of them was a story about a police officer. Police officers make very credible witnesses, and when they say they've seen something you tend to believe them. At one point I even thought the character should be a military person, a debunker working for Project Blue Book' (Bouzereau, 1997).

In fact Spielberg's first approach was to take Hynek's personal biography as the basis for a conspiracy thriller about an official who investigates UFOs in order to debunk them but comes to discover that they actually exist. It is perhaps not surprising that a filmmaker might become attracted to Hynek's story as it provides a dramatic character transformational arc – from sceptic to agnostic to (in Spielberg's version) believer.

Spielberg described his initial pitch as 'UFOs and Watergate', drawing on the idea of the Air Force cover up of the 'truth' about UFOs, and called this first story treatment 'Watch the Skies' (after the warning given at the end of the Howard Hawks/Christian Nyby 1951 sci-fi classic *The Thing from Another World*). (Hynek, for his part, dismisses the suggestion of a conspiracy in *The UFO Experience*, claiming that the lack of interest shown by the United States Air Force towards the UFO phenomenon 'belies any charge of 'cover up'. They just didn't care' [1972: 232].)

Spielberg's producers, Julia and Michael Phillips, brought in Paul Schrader (who had written *Taxi Driver*, which they had produced) to work on the screenplay. One can understand the logic of hiring a writer with an interest in religious transcendence. Schrader had also authored a book on Dreyer, Ozu and Bresson, whose austere 'transcendental style', according to John B. Hamilton, 'resonated with Schrader's Calvinist leanings' (*Senses of Cinema*, 2010).

Schrader and his brother Leonard suggested making the story into a spiritual journey based on the biblical tale of St Paul on the Road to Damascus, whose religious conversion was prompted by the visitation of an angel in the form of a bright white light. The protagonist, a Project Blue Book official like Hynek, would start out as a UFO sceptic until he has his own close encounter that changes his mind. Spielberg, who has always favoured dramatic reversals in his films, was enthusiastic about the idea (indeed, we can see influence of the 'St Paul' scene in the Crescendo Summit sequences of *Close Encounters*; Roy is made a believer by his encounter on the mountain road, and later gathers there with other contactees hoping for a second visitation).

Spielberg had from the start a strong vision of how he wanted the film to end, based on a UFO sighting that supposedly took place in Nuremberg in 1561 (where it was reported that dozens of large, cylindrical objects gathered in the skies, from which many smaller multicoloured objects of different shapes emerged and engaged in battle, as witnessed by the bemused citizens of the medieval town), in a sequence that was to climax with the landing of the giant Mothership:

> I started with the landing, and then tried to back the rest of the story into 'Well, how did they get there? And how can we have an operatic third act encounter between them and us?' (Bouzereau, 2008).

This ending he visualised taking place on a mountain, like the 'Night on Bald Mountain' segment in *Fantasia*. It would be a sublime moment: the Mothership initially envisaged as a hulking dark mass, casting its giant shadow over the mountain.

Therefore, the screenplay that Schrader turned out, entitled, 'Kingdom Come', incorporated, on Spielberg's brief, the phantasmagorical ending, the St Paul-like religious-type conversion of the protagonist that was, in fact, Leonard Schrader's idea (but based on Hynek's own change of heart about the UFO phenomenon), and aspects of witness reports contained in *The UFO Experience* (including the traumatic psychological effects witnesses experienced afterwards, which led in some cases to marriage breakdown and family estrangement).

Schrader's script tells the story of Paul Van Owen, an Air Force officer and Project Blue book official whose job is to debunk UFO sightings on order of the government. One

A production sketch depicting the landing of the Mothership at Devil's Tower.

night, he has a close encounter on a lonely country road that completely changes his belief system. He reports the sighting but his testimony is subjected to ridicule. Growing depressed, his marriage collapses and he becomes isolated from society. Eventually he threatens to expose what he believes is a cover up of the truth by the Air Force. He is approached by a secret government organisation called Project Grief who enlists him to help try to make contact with extraterrestrials. This he attempts to do for fifteen years, before eventually realising that UFOs are really mental projections of 'racial memories' implanted millions of years ago. In order to make 'contact', Van Owen must travel deep into his subconscious and retrieve his alien memory: depicted by Schrader as a simultaneous inner spiritual journey into the collective unconscious and a literal alien encounter taking place on Black Mountain, Idaho. Schrader tells this story in a series of flashbacks as Van Owen prepares to meet the aliens and board the Mothership as an intergalactic missionary.

Opinions vary as to why Spielberg rejected 'Kingdom Come' (despite it containing many elements that would be included in *Close Encounters*). Warren Buckland claims that Spielberg objected to the 'complex achronological structure' that would have slowed down the narrative momentum (2006: 116); Ray Morton observes, 'rather than the requested thriller, Schrader's script turned out to be a dark and, at times, grim supernatural drama with heavy religious overtones' (2007: 66). Spielberg has himself stated that 'Paul went so far away on his own tangent...a terribly guilt-ridden story, not about UFOs at all' (McBride, 1997: 267).

In 1990 Schrader went on record as saying:

> Steven and I had a falling out along strictly ideological lines... What I had done was to write this character with resonances of Lear and St Paul, a kind of Shakespearean tragic hero, and Steven could not get behind that and it became clear that our collaboration had to end. It came down to this. I said, 'I refuse to send off to another world, as the first example of earth's intelligence, a man who wants to go and set up a McDonald's franchise', and Steven said, 'That's exactly the guy I want to send.' Steven's Capra-like infatuation with the common man was diametrically opposed to my religious infatuation with the redeeming hero – I wanted a biblical character to carry the message to the outer spheres, I wanted to form missions again. Fortunately, Steven was smart enough to realise that I was an intractable character and he was right to make the film he was comfortable with. (Jackson, 1990: 125-126)

The Paul Schrader Papers at the University of Texas include notes for a revised draft of 'Kingdom Come' made by Schrader in April, 1974: it is unlikely, therefore, that the 'falling out' between him and Spielberg was an immediate one. However, when Spielberg and Julia and Michael Phillips decided to bring in a new writer – John Hill – to re-write Schrader's draft as a straight thriller, their brief to Hill was, according to him, 'basically similar to the story direction of the Paul Schrader draft: an Air Force officer who is routinely sent out to "investigate" UFO sightings' (Morton, 2007: 70) suggesting that Schrader's account of events might not be entirely accurate, as Spielberg had not yet rethought his protagonist as a 'Capra-like' common man.

Meeting of the Minds

What is clear about the John Hill script, called 'Meeting of the Minds', written in November 1974, is that by that stage in the development process of *Close Encounters*, the basic plot of the film was largely in place.

Hill is probably best known for penning the screenplays to the Andy Kaufmann vehicle *Heartbeeps* (1980) and the Tom Selleck actioner *Quigley Down Under* (1990), as well as such highly successful TV shows as *Quantum Leap* and *L.A. Law*. Back in July 1974, when he was offered the rewrite of *Close Encounters*, Hill was still a largely untested tyro screenwriter working as an advertising copywriter but Julia and Michael Phillips had been impressed by one of his speculatively written screenplays. According to Morton he had, as well, already written a UFO-themed script called 'Something Landed in the North Pasture' (2007: 68).

In Hill's draft the Air Force officer suffers nightmares after his close encounter and begins creating a mountain out of dirt in his living room. As he desperately tries to prove what he saw was real, his home life collapses and his wife leaves. The army try to threaten him into silence. In the meantime, he discovers that a train derailment of nerve gas is really an army cover up (the plot device borrowed from *2001*). Infiltrating the UFO landing site, the officer, in hiding, is vindicated as he witnesses the Mothership land.

By Hill's account, Spielberg already had this basic plot, based on the Schrader draft, but it was left to Hill to piece together what was little more than a series of 'unconnected scenes and ideas...the pieces of this story didn't really fit... certain scenes, like an airplane's encounter with a UFO, and the air traffic controller's confusion, etc., weren't clear to me where they went' (Morton, 2007: 71). Indeed, much of the criticism levelled at the finished film is that it suffers from a somewhat disjointed mid-section ('Mr. Spielberg's usually uncanny cinematic instincts fail him from time to time in the extended central section of the film' reported Vincent Canby in his review for the *New York Times* in 1977). Spielberg concentrated much of his subsequent effort in the writing process, in post-production editing, re-shoots, and – arguably – in revisions made for the *Special Edition* and *Collector's Edition*, trying to solve this problem, unsuccessfully – another reason perhaps why *Close Encounters* remains a 'work in progress'.

Hill wrote a treatment, taking elements from the Schrader draft, and other 'random images and scenes' that he'd been given and tried to give the script 'a beginning, middle and end' (Morton, 2007: 72). Spielberg later commented that 'all of this was out of order in my brain but it found order when I began to write the script from the last scene backwards' (Bouzereau, 2008). Hill also added some of ideas of his own that did not make it into the finished film, such as including an Air Force 'buddy' who tries to help the protagonist prove the existence of UFOs (traces of this idea can be seen in the relationship between Roy and Jillian in the film).

What was still missing in the more tightly structured Hill draft – and this would not come until later, when Spielberg took on the task of writing *Close Encounters* himself – was the crucial 'everyman' protagonist.

When You Wish Upon A Star

Ultimately Spielberg and his producers would decide to drop the 'UFOs and Watergate' conspiracy thriller angle, and with it Hill's script. By the end of 1974, this approach to the material did not seem fresh. Other conspiracy thrillers on studio slates, *The Parallax View*, *Three Days of the Condor* (1975) and *All the President's Men*, were all arisen from Watergate. *Time Out* described the storyline of *The Parallax View* as an 'investigation that reveals a nebulous conspiracy of gigantic and all-embracing scope,' (Glaessner, 1998: 651) which describes well the 1970s conspiracy thriller tropes in general.

It was during post-production on *Jaws* that Spielberg seems to have had his epiphany of making the central character of *Close Encounters* an 'everyman' rather than an Air Force official as he explained:

> … We don't really relate to people in a uniform as rank and file Americans. So I tried to make this person as common as possible. I wanted to make it about me and about my parents and about friends that I knew. I wanted to make it a very accessible story about a common everyday individual who has a sighting that overturns his life as he knew it, and throws his personal life… his family life into complete upheaval as he starts to become more and more obsessed with his experience. (Bouzereau, 1997)

We can sense here a crucial moment of Spielberg finally connecting with the material, finding his own personal affinity with the story. This can, of course, be seen as self-conscious   'auteurism'; Spielberg's moving in the circles of New Hollywood directors – Scorsese, Coppola, De Palma, Milius, Schrader – may have influenced him at this stage in his career in terms of creating an artistic identity. The notion of connecting with the material seems to have been a mantra of New Hollywood. Scorsese, for example, in the 1970s, has also spoken about the need to 'connect with the material', committing to *Raging Bull* only after realising (to sobering effect) that 'the leading character in the film is very similar to me' (Pirie, 1981: 139). Other 'Movie Brat' directors, like De Palma, have often alternated between studio assignments and more personal films (generally ones they originated and wrote themselves). Ray Morton comments that in the case of *Close Encounters*, Spielberg 'knew he wanted to humanize the story, to make it warmer and personal. He also wanted to capture the magic and wonder of UFOs and of outer space, elements he felt were missing in (previous drafts)' (2007, 77). This idea of personalising a film was also, of course, a way for New Hollywood directors to distinguish themselves from the 'hard-hatted journeymen' that they superseded in the eyes of the studios; New Hollywood directors often provided the X-factor box office successes (*The Godfather* [1972], *The Exorcist* [1973], *Jaws*, *Star Wars*) where other journeymen hard-hats (*Lucky Lady* [1975], *King Kong* [1976], *Meteor* [1979]) failed.

The 'Spielberg touch' is thought to derive from his ability to elicit emotion in the audience via their identification with his characters – a largely improvisatory skill as a director for which he has been both praised and criticised. 'I wouldn't be satisfied with my films if there weren't human beings functioning as your guide through this world of mechanized madness,' Spielberg commented in 1978 (Tuchman, 1978: 44). When asked how he achieved this, he replied, 'Just by placing myself, Steve Spielberg, in the situation and saying, "What would I do?". Thus, in *Jaws*, Hooper's ridiculous comeback at Quint, his squeezing the Styrofoam cup in response to Quint's crushing the beer can, was a Spielberg improvisation based on his thinking "If I were Hooper, how would I get back at Quint?" Likewise, in the same film, the striking scene where Brody's brooding gestures in his kitchen are mimicked by his young son is a typical Spielberg 'soft moment', another improvisation designed to humanise his characters. 'It's little things like that that I'm able to interject in terms of humanizing my movies,' (ibid., 45).

Close Encounters, then, came to be structured around these 'soft moments', around emotion. *Close Encounters* inspires feelings of awe and wonder – no question – but also feelings of enchantment, sadness and, sometimes, fear. Emotion – our ability to feel – and emotion as concomitant to communication (whatever language is used) is inherent in the film's intended meaning:

> Everything [in the script] is for an emotional reason; it's not really a mechanical reason at all. I mean that's what all film is: all the prismatic images in the motion picture are solicitous of a visceral response from people who are looking at the overall movie. (Tuchman, 1978: 44)

Spielberg's approach to the filmmaking process is to structure emotions in a way similar to music. Indeed he claims that 'the whole movie' of *Close Encounters* came from a song: 'When You Wish Upon a Star' from Pinocchio, 'and the feeling the song gave me when I was a kid listening to it. The song meant stars, magic' (Hodenfield, 1978: 36). Ultimately he hung the story 'on the mood the song created, the way it affected me emotionally' (McBride, 1997: 262).

Thus, *Close Encounters* begins (and ends) with Spielbergian 'exultaté'.

Close Encounters: Production

The long-drawn-out filming of *Close Encounters* commenced mid-May 1976 at Devil's Tower, Wyoming (substantial accounts exist of the production [see Morton, Balaban, McBride, Crawley etc.] so basic details will suffice here). The Wyoming sequences, including Roy and Jillian's cross-country drive and seeing the Tower for the first time; their subsequent capture and escape from the evacuation helicopter; and their scramble up the Devil's Tower to the UFO landing site were all filmed on location (the final section of the chase up the mountain was filmed on a set), as were the evacuation camp scenes featuring Lacombe, Neary, Laughlin and Major Walsh.

The production company relocated to Mobile, Alabama at the end of May 1976, where the majority of the film was shot between May and August. A giant set (at the time, the largest ever constructed for a film) of the Box Canyon landing site was erected in an aircraft hangar at Brookley Field Airforce Base, outside of Mobile. The

Close Encounters pressbook reveals the magnitude of this set and its construction requirements:

> The hangar measured 450 feet long, 250 feet wide and 90 feet high. Its conversion and construction of the sets demanded staggering amounts of varied materials. They included: 54,000 board feet (approximately 10 miles) of lumber; 19,000 feet of steel scaffolding, 29, 500 feet of nylon canopy, 16,900 feet of fiberglass, two miles of steel cable, 5000 yards of cloth backing, 150 tons of air conditioning, 26,000 square yards of terrace concrete slabs and 7000 yards of sand and clay fill dirt. A total of 885 cubic yards of concrete fill were used. Enough to build a structure comparable in size to the Washington Monument. (Columbia Pictures, 1977)

As well as filming the final climactic encounter here, a second smaller set was constructed in another hangar at the base for the Crescendo Summit sequences. A tract house in the suburbs outside Mobile (which resembled suburban housing in the midwest setting of the film) was the location for the scenes set in and around Roy's home. Similarly, a farmhouse near the town of Fairhope, Alabama, off Highway 181 was used for the interiors and exteriors of Jillian's home. Also filmed on location in Alabama, were Roy's encounter in his truck and the airforce debunking scenes.

After a hiatus of two months production recommenced in Los Angeles in December 1976 (with John A. Alonzo replacing Vilmos Zsigmond as cinematographer) to film the UFO police chase sequences. Another break in filming further truncated the production; Director of Photography Douglas Slocombe was recruited for the India sequence, shot on location in Mumbai between February 24-26, 1977.

Post-production commenced on Spielberg's return to Los Angeles, where he supervised Trumbull's work on the Special Visual Effects, whilst editing the film with Michael Kahn in a rented apartment close to Trumbull's Marina Del Rey production facility where the effects work was taking place. After screening the rough cut to Columbia executives, the studio granted Spielberg further funds to shoot additional sequences. These included the film's opening Flight 19 section; the scene at Goldstone Deep Space Communications Complex where Laughlin deciphers the mysterious signal as map co-ordinates; and the final greeting between Lacombe and the lone extraterrestrial. All were shot in Los Angeles in May 1977.

'Not since DeMille': The giant Close Encounters *set.*

Truffaut, Balaban, Lance Henrickson,Spielberg and Zsigmond (l-r) on set.

The film's first release took place in December 1977 at a final negative cost (before marketing and promotion) of $19.4 million.

Special Edition

Spielberg famously returned to *Close Encounters* before its planned re-release in 1980, and secured additional funds from Columbia in order to shoot new sequences that he had been forced to delete from the original script originally due to escalating production costs. These included the discovery in the Gobi desert of the S.S. Cotopaxi (a tramp steamer ship that had disappeared in 1925 supposedly in the Bermuda Triangle) and a scene taking us inside the Mothership as Neary enters it at the end of the film. Both were included in the *Special Edition* of *Close Encounters* (as well as some added shots in Roy's initial encounter scene), but both are arguably redundant. Spielberg removed the scene of Roy inside the Mothership from the *Collector's Edition*, admitting that its inclusion had been a mistake on his part and that what happens after Roy enters is best left to the imagination (Bouzereau, 2007).

3. *Close Encounters*: Analysis

Let There Be Light

The preview audience attending the special advance screening of *Close Encounters of the Third Kind* at the Zeigfeld Theater, 141 West 54th Street in Manhattan on Sunday 6th November, 1977, were, according to critic Roger Ebert, expecting to be disappointed. Advance word was that the movie would bomb, taking the debt-ridden Columbia Pictures along with it. To say that Spielberg and Columbia had a lot riding on the film would be somewhat of an understatement.

Amongst the cast and crew at the screening (which did not include a nervous Spielberg, who waited it out in his hotel room) was Bob Balaban who plays the interpreter, David Laughlin. In his *Close Encounters of the Third Kind Diary*, Balaban describes for us in detail the fraught circumstances of this, the film's first public showing:

> Columbia's campaign of secrecy before the movie's opening has begun to backfire, and the press is getting a little hostile. *New York Magazine* sneaked someone into a Dallas preview and has printed a rotten review. Columbia stock dropped so quickly that trading had to be stopped...The film is opening six months later than predicted, and came in nine million dollars over budget. And there is some fear that *Star Wars* may have stolen its thunder. (1978: 173)

Of the atmosphere in the auditorium as lights slowly dimmed and the opening titles came on screen, Ebert wrote:

> There was a certain hush: Here was director Steven Spielberg's $24-million gamble, and we were about to see if he'd pulled it off...

But the critics and the naysayers had not counted on Spielberg's mastery of light and sound, his ability to mesmerise and disarm audiences through the medium of cinema. (*Close Encounters* was one of the first films [along with *Tommy* [1975] and *Star Wars*] to utilise the Dolby Sound System; both the Ziegfeld Theater and the Cinerama Dome Theater in Los Angeles, where *Close Encounters* received its premiere engagements, presented the film in 70mm, six-track Dolby stereo.)

Ebert goes on:

> Suddenly, blindingly, the theater was filled with sound and light: with a dazzling white flash from the screen, and a powerful musical chord so loud on the Dolby stereo system that we felt a wall of air against our faces. In that masterstroke in his first few frames of film, Spielberg laid bold claim to his audience...the slate was wiped clean by Spielberg's unearthly opening blast of sound and light... (Ebert, 1977)

According to Balaban:

> There is a blinding flash and a thunderous clap of music; at that moment you can feel the audience getting hooked. There's a great feeling of relief in the theatre – Spielberg's done it again. (1978: 174)

Close Encounters opens with white credits on a black background, accompanied by a crescendo of strings and choir by John Williams. The first credit informs us that this is 'a Columbia Presentation in Association with EMI', significant in that Columbia had to secure outside investment in order to raise nine million dollars of the film's budget; EMI (along with Time Warner Inc.) made up the financial shortfall.

Next comes the film's title, in mysterious 'shuttered' letters telling us that this is a science fiction film, but keeping us guessing as to the exact meaning of the words: what are 'close encounters of the third kind'? Although the term 'close encounter' has since entered the language – it's even in the *Oxford English Dictionary* ('a supposed encounter with a UFO or with aliens') – back in 1977 the phrase was little known. As a film title 'Close Encounters of the Third Kind' was actually quite problematic. Screenwriter (and advertising copywriter) John Hill objected to it, claiming it was a 'blind title' – 'no-one knows what it means until AFTER they buy the product' (Morton, 2007: 71). Spielberg himself had a hard time selling the title to Columbia's marketing department; and in preparation for the film's release, the studio had to run adverts in newspapers and magazines explaining it to the public, using a simplified version of Hynek's definitions of the three different kinds of close encounters (ibid., 291). In *Aliens* (1986) director James Cameron pays homage to Spielberg's film by having one of his characters brandish a shot gun that he carries especially 'for close encounters'. Even today, audiences new to the film and weaned on movies like *Independence Day* are liable to be sorely disappointed by its lack of hand-to-hand combat with the ETs – something that the title surely promises!

Then in the credits come the stars of the show – Julia and Michael Phillips, Dreyfuss, Truffaut, Zsigmond – and perhaps the film's biggest star – Spielberg himself. Spielberg is awarded a writer-director credit, although several others beside Paul Schrader and John Hill worked on the script, unaccredited. These were David Giler, Jerry Belson and Hal Barwood & Matthew Robbins. More will be said about some of their contributions later. Spielberg's solo credit is perhaps the result of ego, but also speaks of the film's personal nature to the director.

We hold on 20 seconds of black screen; the Williams score builds slowly, ethereally, promising mystery and the sublime. Like Méliès, Spielberg is a master illusionist of the cinema, one of its great magicians. He makes us wait for cinema's very essence: *light*. And then gives it to us suddenly in a blinding flash, achieved by inserting two frames of white leader before the first image. (Spielberg's use of the cinematic apparatus in *Close Encounters* has received significant critical attention; see, for example, Morris, 2007: 8-19.)

Of the booming music chord that opens the film in accompaniment to the blinding white flash, Spielberg has revealed, 'that was a 'C' Major chord. Nothing else would have had that impact, that rush of air' (Ebert, 1977). Combined, the two produce Spielberg's desired effect of what he called 'wow-ness'.

Spielberg and Thalberg

Speaking in 1983, Spielberg remarked that directors such as himself and George Lucas 'would like to do to the film industry what Irving Thalberg did to it fifty years ago' (Crawley, 1983: 39). In some ways we can see the partial fulfilment of this ambition in his subsequent diversification into producing films directed by others. In many instances those films were developed by Spielberg and his production company, Amblin Entertainment, for Spielberg to direct, and then passed on to other directors at a late stage in their development. Films like *The Goonies, Back to the Future* and *Young Sherlock Holmes* (all 1985), for example, seem to be more recognisably 'Spielberg' films than trademarks of Richard Donner, Robert Zemeckis and Barry Levinson. Spielberg, as producer, undoubtedly exercised a high level of creative control over these films even if he did not actually direct them, the way that Thalberg, as supervising producer, steered many of his productions at Universal and later MGM in the 1920s-1930s.

Moreover, Spielberg, like Thalberg before him, sees the completed film as raw material. After sneak previews, Thalberg would order entire scenes reshot and alter endings for greater audience appeal (Balio, 1985: 264). Spielberg would do the same for his films, particularly *Close Encounters*, for which he would restructure and shoot new footage throughout post-production, right up until the film's premiere (and beyond, in the *Special Edition*). Balaban remarks of the film's delayed premiere:

> The opening kept getting postponed because Spielberg was changing things. Small things: an added closeup of a Jiminy Cricket figurine in Richard Dreyfuss's den, inserts of hands opening doors, things like that. (1978: 173)

Spielberg has spoken of the preview-retake system pioneered by Irving Thalberg, adopted by Hollywood in the 1930s, and embraced by Spielberg decades later, in these terms:

> I have previewed a film and revised it, juxtaposed certain things and deleted or even extended certain moments. I use previews the way theatrical directors use rehearsals. They listen to the reactions; they change things. If there is a huge laugh and pertinent dialogue is about to occur they'll hold for the laughter. I use previews that way. The difference is, there's a lot more time in theatre than there is in film. When you get down to the preview stage, there's probably about three weeks left to do everything before the film is released. (Royal, 1982: 97)

The opening scene is a case in point. Not featured in the original script, Spielberg wrote it, together with Hal Barwood & Matthew Robbins, after principle photography had been completed and a first cut of the film made by editor, Michael Kahn. An informal preview screening to friends and associates revealed certain deficiencies in the film, as Spielberg notes:

The whole film was cut together and the cut, I realized, was five or six scenes too short. Not that the movie was too short but that there were scenes that just didn't give you enough mystery, enough 'wow'. Not enough 'wow' at the beginning. (Bouzereau, 1997)

In fact, Spielberg's working method during *Close Encounters* involved editing the film as shooting proceeded during principal photography. Not an uncommon practice as it enables a director and editor to see how well the film is cutting together as they go along, and, if necessary, to reshoot or add new material ('pick ups', 'cut-ins', 'cutaways' etc.) while cast and crew are still assembled. (Morton, 2007: 254). Spielberg, however, kept *Close Encounters* in a state of flux to an unusual degree throughout the filming stage and into post-production. There is no sense of him, for example, locking down the script before filming commenced and then 'shooting the script as written', because the script, to all intents and purposes, was never really finalised; the shooting draft screenplay of *Close Encounters* (dated 14th May, 1976) therefore does not function as a blue print of the movie, only as a rough sketch that would be much revised and embellished in the making of the film. During shooting, Michael Kahn would assemble preliminary versions of each scene in an editing facility housed on location, and Spielberg would enhance and clarify these scenes with extra footage: an organic method of working and one that Spielberg would continue after principal photography and into post-production as well.

Editor, Michael Kahn on location with Spielberg.

As Michael Kahn fine-tuned the first cut, interweaving the various subplots, a number of scenes were deleted in order to better structure the film. One of those scenes was the initial meeting between Truffaut's character, Claude Lacombe, and his interpreter, Laughlin, which, in the script, takes place at an airport during the investigation of a close encounter between a passenger airliner and a UFO. Balaban reports that the scene was 'too static' and that Spielberg decided to film a new introduction between the two characters that would become the opening scene (1978: 157). A comparison of the deleted scene and the revised version that opens *Close Encounters* clearly illustrates what Spielberg meant by the film needing more 'wow'.

Deleted Airport Scene

The deleted airport scene, available as an extra in the *Collector's Edition* DVD of *Close Encounters*, is indeed static and dull, as Balaban notes. Partly this is because Spielberg covers the scene in a highly conventional way as a series of shot/reverse shots (Buckland, 2006: 116). Interestingly, this is the way dialogue scenes are typically filmed in television, as static 'talking heads'; a code that Spielberg declined to follow earlier in his career when he was a director working in television:

> The one thing I refused to conform to was the television formula of closeup, two-shot, over the-shoulders and master shot...I considered each show a mini-feature and I would shoot it as I would shoot a feature. (Poster, 1978: 65)

Unfortunately this scene conforms almost entirely to the episodic television way of shooting, possibly because Spielberg's options are severely limited by the nature of the scene; most of it takes place within the confined space of a limousine inside which Lacombe asks his new interpreter to read from a pornographic novel, to see if he is able to translate words of 'emotional value'. Spielberg tries to introduce a sense of excitement and mystery by intercutting Laughlin's interview with what is taking place on the passenger airliner; we see an Air Force official attempt to confiscate cameras and rolls of film from passengers who may have photographed the UFO. This intercutting doesn't really work, however, and the overall effect is clumsy. The scene has the look and feel of a Paramount *Airport* movie (*Airport* [1970], *Airport 1975*

The deleted airport scene.

[1974], *Airport '77* [1977], *Airport '80: The Concorde* [1980] – memorably spoofed in *Airplane* [1980]) – another reason why Spielberg may have deleted it. Moreover, as Buckland points out, the scene delivers a lacklustre introduction to Truffaut's character (2006: 116) – and Balaban's for that matter.

There *is* an intriguing reference to the Wright-Patterson Air Force Base in the scene. Laughlin, it is revealed, has been with the Mayflower project for two years, at the Wright-Paterson Facility in Dayton, Ohio, the site of Hanger 18, which allegedly houses evidence from the Roswell UFO Incident (and provided the title for cheap knockoff UFO movie *Hanger 18* [1980]). There he transcribed 'sleep tape'. When Laughlin asks his new superior why he chose a dirty book for translation, Lacombe replies, 'there is a connection in all languages between expressed feelings and the very nature of language'. We might read this as a philosophical aside on the film's theme of 'communication across barriers, which is most explicitly manifest, of course, in the film's final moments, as humans and aliens communicate with one another through the language of music.' (Buckland, 2006: 116) (In *E.T.* Spielberg makes it clear that the telepathic link between human and E.T. is primarily an emotional one: 'Elliott thinks its thoughts.' 'No, Elliott feels his feelings.') Overall, however, the scene lacks any sense of Spielbergian 'wowness'.

Instead, what Spielberg gives us in the revised opening scene of *Close Encounters*, added late in the production, is spectacle akin that of the *Indiana Jones* quadrilogy: planes, sandstorms, a stirring Williams score, mystery and occultism (Flight 19/ Ark of the Covenant: both of them are mystical and 'lost'). Britton's observation that

Spielberg's cynicism and sincerity 'consort quite naturally with each other' springs to mind here: this is a popcorn entertainment opening, no question. In contrast with the grittier New Hollywood realism of Vilmos Zsigmond's work in the majority of *Close Encounters*, even William A. Fraker's cinematography lends a dash of traditional Hollywood razzle-dazzle (and anticipates the polished look that Spielberg, and other directors like Ridley Scott, would become known for in the 1980s). As an overture it may be vacuous – compared to say, The Dawn of Man sequence in *2001* – but as an audience attention grabber it is text book and, again, is worth analysing in detail for this reason.

'Are We the First?'

The blinding flash of light after the credits quickly leads to the disorientation of a violent sand storm. A subtitle informs that were are in the Sonora Desert in Mexico and that it is present day (the sequence was actually filmed in California's Mojave Desert, an hour's drive from Los Angeles – a typical example of Hollywood illusionism).

A jeep's headlights come into view as the vehicle fights sand and wind. A team of men disembark, including J. Patrick McNamara as the Project leader (a role vastly expanded from that of the screenplay during shooting), goggled up and holding handkerchiefs to their faces. As McNamara advances alongside a fence (a similar shot features in the opening scene of *Jaws* where Chrissie (Susan Backlinie) traverses sand dunes to the sea and her doom), the camera tracks with him past abandoned cars – are we in a junkyard? Spielberg utilises what Buckland terms 'slow disclosure' at the start of the sequence, only gradually establishing the geography of the scene. The effect is disorientating, akin to us entering a strange land.

We see from McNamara's point of view a toothless Mexican army officer and his men waiting a few metres away – the reverse tracking shot towards him further evoking this sense of a mysterious journey embarked upon. Dario Argento opens his Euro-horror classic *Suspiria* (1977) in a similar way, with the same configuration of shot/reverse-point of view shot tracking Suzie Bannion (Jessica Harper) as she leads us into an arcane world of magic and witchcraft. Christopher Vogler speaks of this kind of disorientating prologue as leading to suggestibility – the audience will be more psychologically open to story events that strain credibility if they are first thrown a little off-base and their normal perceptions upset. The opening of *Close Encounters* does precisely this, as Vogler explains: Spielberg 'intrigues the audience with a host of riddles, and gives a foretaste of the thrills and wonder ahead.' The scene acts as a form of initiation ceremony for the audience whereby they are metaphorically 'blindfolded and led around in the dark' until 'they begin to suspend their disbelief and enter more readily into a special world of fantasy' (1996: 100-101).

We cut back to McNamara and his initial line of dialogue is suitably cryptic: 'Are we the first?' The camera continues to track backwards to bring two more soldiers into view, and we then have a group formation. Spielberg utilises the technique of overlapping dialogue to further disorientate the viewer (some reviewers found this technique, used at various stages throughout the film, off-putting: 'an almost nonstop confusion of voices, languages, technical jargon, weather, vehicles and [I sometimes suspect] gibberish, often so noisy that you can't hear yourself think' [Canby, 1977]). The violence of the sand storm forces the Americans and Mexicans to shout in order to make themselves heard and even then they struggle to understand each other because of the language barrier: a motif that introduces the film's central theme of 'communication across divides' (Buckland, 2006: 116) more effectively than in the deleted airport scene.

A second car arrives and a further group of scientists emerge. 'Is the interpreter with you?' McNamara asks. Enter Laughlin, bustling into close-up, bearded and bespectacled. Throughout the scene, Spielberg keeps the camera low, framing characters against a sky as ominous as the ocean in *Jaws*. From his dramatic entrance we would presume Balaban the protagonist. Audiences in 1977 might indeed have thought him Dreyfuss: the physical similarity between them is marked – he looks very much like Dreyfuss in *Jaws*. Spielberg cast Balaban after seeing him in *Midnight Cowboy* (1969) in which he plays a timid student eager for the attentions of Jon Voight's Stetson-hatted hustler. According to Morton, Spielberg was pleased with Balaban's performance during principal photography of *Close Encounters* and wanted to give him more to do (2007: 258). Additional scenes were written that allowed

Laughlin more of a character arc. In an intriguing mirroring of Roy Neary, Laughlin is presented as a milquetoast who must distinguish himself from the rank and file within the Mayflower project. We see him grow in confidence and importance throughout the film. It is Laughlin who, using his skills as a cartographer, cracks the code of the UFO landing site, identifying numbers as map co-ordinates, thus enabling first contact with the extraterrestrials, and earning his place at Devil's Tower with the others. Like Roy Neary, David Laughlin, by the end of the *Close Encounters*, achieves self-actualisation. Balaban would go on to play similar roles in Ken Russell's science fiction drama *Altered States* (1980) and Peter Hyams's sequel to Kubrick's classic, *2010* (1984), before making his feature directing debut in the underrated cannibal black comedy *Parents* (1989) and helming episodes of such cult Sci-Fi/fantasy television shows as *Tales from the Darkside*, *Amazing Stories* and *Eerie, Indiana*.

Truffaut

François Truffaut's Lacombe is introduced in equally dynamic manner. McNamara, Balaban and the others are grouped in front of wooden arch entrance to the junkyard. It is the first shot of the film that clearly establishes the space. From the back of the frame, where he has stood unnoticed, Truffaut marches over to greet Laughlin. No longer the limousine lizard of the deleted airport scene, the new Lacombe is a dashing khaki-clad explorer with tousled grey hair and aviator shades. The camera dollies in from the wide shot to frame a close-up of Truffaut over Balaban's shoulder; Spielberg fawns over Truffaut in this scene, emphasising in reverent close-up his benign authority. In casting Truffaut, Spielberg had been attracted to the performances that the French director had given in his own films, in particular, *L'Enfant Sauvage* (1970), in which Truffaut had played a compassionate doctor treating a feral child: 'I needed a man who would have the soul of a child, someone kindly, warm, who completely accepts the extraordinary, the irrational', Spielberg has remarked (De Baecque and Toubiana, 1999: 325). Although Truffaut had apparently little interest in the subject of UFOs, it is possible he recognised a kinship of sorts with Spielberg which persuaded him to accept the role. Truffaut had already adapted Ray Bradbury's classic of humanist 'soft' science fiction, *Fahrenheit 451* for the screen in

François Truffaut as Claude Lacombe.

1966, and may have recognised the Bradbury influence in Spielberg's script.

As Laughlin and Lacombe meet for the first time, the various groups of men merge into one. Convergence as a motif plays out in the film as a whole in the interweaving of the three main plotlines – Roy's UFO odyssey, Jillian's search for her abducted son and Lacombe & Laughlin's investigation. These three plotlines conjoin at Devil's Mountain, subsumed in turn by the coming together of humans and extraterrestrials in a meeting of the minds.

Spielberg's Use of Long Takes

'They're all there. All of them!' With these words, imparted by a member of the Mayflower team, Spielberg moves us into the second part of the sequence, increasing the mystery and amping up the 'wowness'. Next comes an impressive piece of staging for the camera, made all the more so by the fact that it goes virtually unnoticed by the viewer, who is by now caught up in (Spielberg's detractors might say rendered uncritical by) the mystery and the excitement of the unfolding drama. It is also one of several plan séquence shots in *Close Encounters* that demonstrate Spielberg's skill in heightening the emotion of a scene through camera movement.

As the Mayflower team move into the junkyard Spielberg uses a tracking shot to slowly reveal a group of five tornado bombers positioned in a circle in the yard. Team-members weave past the camera inspecting each plane in turn; we follow them in an anti-clockwise movement until we reach the last bomber, where Lacombe and Laughlin emerge from beneath a wing in the *opposite direction* and walk toward the camera into close up. The scene's energy is generated by the combination of Williams's driving music, the balletic choreography of the camera and performers and the unexpected reveal of the five bombers. Moreover, Spielberg's use of the camera remains unobtrusive. Despite the complexity of the shot we do not notice the camera because we are drawn in by the urgency of the scene, its suspense and its enigma. Spielberg's skill in mobile mise-en-scène developed in television, partly as a result of his afore-mentioned refusal to conform to televisual codes and partly out of pragmatism:

> I'd have 25 shots prepared for one day and wound up doing eleven. And because of the schedule, I wound up shooting scenes in one shot, and began working in long continuous masters letting the camera follow the people, without covering, which got me into trouble very early in TV. One day I directed a *Night Gallery* and I had to get eight pages out in that one day. So I did the eight pages in one shot... The shot was very involved; it went through two rooms, characters went into close-ups and out of close-ups and talked far and close, but never calling attention to the camera. I think it was plotted out in such a way that you were never aware of the moving camera. (Bacher, 1978: 186-7)

The long take is a Spielberg staple: examples exist in each of his films, but it is an aspect of his work rarely commented upon, possibly because his plan séquences are characterised by their very invisibility – the way he moves his actors and follows them with a fluid moving camera that in essence links together a number of shots into one. The effect of the long take on the viewer is to draw us into the scene, increasing emotional involvement; and this reflects, as we already know, Spielberg's essentially intuitive approach to filmmaking. Arguably, the plan séquence shots in *Close Encounters* are some of the most effective of Spielberg's career for this reason.

The Missing Flight 19

Spielberg builds true life phenomena into *Close Encounters* from the opening scene where we are informed that the bombers are in fact the missing Flight 19: military aircraft that disappeared over the Atlantic whilst on a training mission in December 1945. Flight 19 has been described as one of the great aviation mysteries of all time and popularised the myth of the Bermuda Triangle, an area between Bermuda, Florida and Puerto Rico in which a number of ships and aircraft have vanished without trace or explanation. Author Charles Berlitz's 1974 best-seller *The Bermuda Triangle* (adapted into a film of the same name in 1978) posited several outlandish theories for these disappearances, one of which is, of course, abduction by aliens. Part of the appeal of *Close Encounters* for audiences of the time was the way it keyed into the public's fascination with this kind of strange phenomena in the 1970s. That decade saw the biggest wave of UFO sightings since the 1950s, a worldwide resurgence of interest in UFOlogy and a UFO abduction cult that continues to this day (especially in parts of California where radio shows like *California MUFON Radio* are devoted to abductees telling their stories). The American obsession with government-cover ups and UFOs can in itself be seen as part of a wider obsession with the occult, witchcraft, ESP, mind-control, herbal medicines, religious cultism, and such radical therapies as bioenergetics, gestalt and primal scream therapy (Van Wert, 1974: 5).

Scholar Joseph Laycock has described the public obsession with all things paranormal in the 1970s as 'folk-piety' – 'an appealing alternative to rationalised religion and a secular social order' (2009: 2-27). For many, such films as *The Exorcist* (1973) and *Close Encounters*, particularly at the time of their release, provided a mystical, quasi-religious experience in an age of declining church attendance and increasing material discontent. 'People are always looking for – I don't know what you'd call it – I guess, the cosmic entertainment', Spielberg observed in 1977 (Combs: 30). Here again, in that last quote, we might see another example of Spielberg's consorting cynicism and sincerity. Critics of Spielberg have accused the film of cashing in on 'The Spiritual Supermarket of America' (Gordon, 1980: 156-7); whilst others allow that *Close Encounters* follows in a tradition of marvellous narratives that, from the outset, present Otherness within the context of 'supernatural qualities' (Telotte, 2001: 147). Laycock makes the point that, in fact, modern American religion can be thought of as 'a sort of dialectic between formal religion and extra-ecclesiastical religion or folk piety' (2009: 3).

The third section of the opening sequence cements a sense of such mysteries unexplained. The Mexican officer leads Lacombe, Laughlin and the McNamara character to a cantina near the junkyard, where an old local man sits in a trance-like state. We are told that the elderly Señor may have witnessed the strange events that took place the previous night. The camera moves in closer as we await explanation. The kindly Lacombe cups the old man's chin and raises him from his stupor. 'Sunburn?' Truffaut asks, in his heavy accent, of the man's red, burned face: a physical after-effect of a close encounter that will become significant later in the story. In Mexican-Spanish the old man delivers the final 'zinger', revealing to McNamara that 'the sun came out last night' and sang to him. Lacombe looks to Laughlin for the translation from English to French, and we have another plan séquence that heightens the emotions of the scene. The camera pans to Laughlin silhouetted against the dusty sky – and tracks in slowly to him as he completes the translation. He backs away from the others and the camera continues to move with him. Clearly unsettled, he looks tentatively up at the sky, as the sandstorm obliterates our view of him and creates a physical fade out of the scene. Whatever one's ideological view of Spielberg, it is difficult to imagine a sequence more effective in conveying that sense of fascination with strange phenomena in the 1970s. It is the crowning moment of Spielbergian 'wow', in an opening scene of 'wow-ness.'

Vilmos Zsigmond and the New Hollywood of the 1970s

Spielberg's collaboration with Hungarian-born cinematographer Zsigmond on *Close Encounters* (and *The Sugarland Express*) links Spielberg interestingly to the New Hollywood of the 1970s, primarily through Zsigmond's early work with director Robert Altman. Indeed, Spielberg chose Zsigmond for *The Sugarland Express* having been impressed by his distinctive cinematography for *McCabe and Mrs Miller* (1971). As already noted, Spielberg associated with a number of New Hollywood directors in the early 70s – Coppola, De Palma, Scorsese and Michael Ritchie, (director of the social satires, *The Candidate* [1972], *Prime Cut* [1972], *Smile* [1975] as well as the sports films, *Downhill Racer* [1969], *The Bad-News Bears* [1976] and *Semi-Tough* [1977]; Spielberg was himself attached to direct the baseball comedy-drama, *The*

Bingo Long Travelling All-Stars and Motor Kings [John Badham, 1976] prior to *Close Encounters*). Lesser known perhaps is that Spielberg helped develop the screenplay of Robert Altman's classic gambling movie *California Split* (1974) alongside writer Joseph Walsh with a view to directing it, before leaving the project to pursue *The Sugarland Express* instead; the script was then offered to Altman. Spielberg seems to have remained a fan of Altman during the 70s, however; referring in interviews to the older director's freewheeling style of directing actors, and utilising Altman-type improvisation techniques in his own films, including in *Close Encounters*:

> We would find the theme of each scene, we would do improvisations about that theme (I had a tape-recorder running), then I'd quickly run to the typewriter, find the best lines, and rewrite the scene so that the next morning the actors had a written script based on some loose improvisations the night before. (Combs, 1977: 34)

It seems inevitable, then, that Spielberg would seek out Altman's principal cameraman, who through his work with these two directors, and other so-called '70s mavericks – John Boorman, Peter Fonda, Michael Cimino and Jerry Schatzberg – might be seen as instrumental in formulating the New Hollywood's visual aesthetic.

Vilmos Zsigmond and Spielberg line up a shot on location.

As a cinematographer, Zsigmond preferred a fast and loose way of working, and had a reputation for achieving striking location photography using mainly natural and available light. New Hollywood directors favoured the realism of filming on location as opposed to in a studio, although this posed challenges for controlling lighting as Zsigmond explains:

> [W]hen Altman decided to do those kind of pictures and some of the younger directors decided to go that way, basically it was against the establishment, against the old Hollywood style...That's the beautiful thing about realistic pictures versus old Hollywood: we utilise locations...[but] the lighting is much more difficult on location than on a stage. So we have to work much harder to give the feeling that you are seeing the real thing. (Shaefer and Salvato, 1984: 313)

In *McCabe and Mrs Miller*, Zsigmond used a photographic technique known as 'flashing', whereby the negative is pre-exposed and later force-developed by the lab in order to facilitate filming in low levels of light. At the same time, flashing the negative created sepia colour tones, like faded old photographs, that suited Altman's elegiac anti-western stylistically. In films like *Deliverance* (1971), *Scarecrow* (1973) *The Sugarland Express* (1974), *The Deerhunter* (1978), Zsigmond went for a vivid harder-edged look that reflected the contemporary working class milieu of the main characters. Zsigmond and Spielberg adopt this approach in *Close Encounters*, particularly in the early scenes, which highlight, as Stephen Rowley notes, 'an affinity with the gritty, working class realities of the New Hollywood of the 1970s' (*Senses of Cinema*, 2006).

Nowhere is this more apparent than in the second scene of the film, where Zsigmond's use of available light, shallow focus and location shooting (in a real air traffic control centre in Palmdale, California) helps lend an air of workplace authenticity to a sequence depicting a radar visual sighting of a UFO (based on the eyewitness reports in Hynek's *The UFO Experience*). What makes this scene particularly interesting in the context of New Hollywood cinema is that it is one of several in *Close Encounters* to show the impact of the UFO visitation on the rank and file worker, whether it be an air traffic controller, a power company operative, a police officer, soldier or government scientist. A dovetailing of New Hollywood sensibilities and Spielberg's imperative a' la Hynek, 'to attempt to portray the kinds of things that people – real everyday human beings with jobs and families – say they have actually experienced'. In the words of screenwriter and blogger, Todd Alcott: 'it's a scene about a bunch of professionals talking on radios and yet somehow the tension is palpable.' The plausibility of the scene arises from the casting of unknown actors delivering authentic jargon of the workplace; 'the performances deriving their power from what the characters are *not* saying, not what they *are* saying', as Alcott notes (July, 2008).

Air Traffic Control detect a UFO by radar.

Spielberg withholds more than he shows – we are not permitted to see the UFOs for ourselves as sighted by the pilots of the passenger jets. Instead we are kept in the confined space of the air traffic control centre, with the voices of the pilots describing the close encounter to the sector controller, Harry Crain (played by David Anderson, a real life air traffic controller with the Federal Aviation Administration). Zsigmond's camera remains on the faces of Harry and the other controllers throughout, only occasionally cutting away to Harry's reflection in the radar and to the scope which shows the planes as blocks of data. Zsigmond filmed the scene using only available light, with the camera lens wide open, giving an extremely shallow depth of field. This contributes immensely to the claustrophobic intensity of the scene as only part of the shot is in clear focus and the background becomes a blur of neon-lit faces. In a masterly use of shallow focus to heighten tension, Zsigmond tracks the camera back from Harry to reveal the other controllers, shifting focus as each comes into frame. At the same time, Spielberg has the actors overlap their dialogue Altman-style. The camera then reverses direction, tracking *forward* into Harry, as a collision between Aireast 31 and the UFO seems imminent. Other workers gradually group around Harry as the scene builds, listening intently. Finally, after the UFO takes off in a vertical direction (as in Hynek's book) Harry asks each of the pilots if he wants to make a report.

Alcott remarks that it is hard to imagine Spielberg directing a scene like this today, one that is all subtlety and nuance, and one that would probably be cut from any movie made in Hollywood in 2015. And yet it remains a perfectly realised scene: Zsigmond's cinematography lending verisimilitude and intimacy; taking inspiration from limitation. It was actually the first scene filmed, shot in December 1975, six months before principal photography commenced, while the script was still being worked on. Columbia had needed *Close Encounters* to be officially 'in production' before the end of 1975 in order to claim tax shelter money for the film. It was also originally intended to be the opening scene of the film but was deemed by Spielberg a weak way to begin the movie after the first cut was put together (Morton, 2007: 257).

Star Children

The action shifts to a remote farmhouse in Muncie, Indiana. Spielberg frames a tight close up of a child sleeping. The close shot of his cherubic face takes on an iconic quality. In *Close Encounters* the camera repeatedly finds child-like faces young and old alike, holding on them, tracking into them. 'The inner child' is a key theme of *Close Encounters*, central to its message; we can see Barry Guiler (played by Cary Guffey) therefore as symbolic of 'the uneducated innocence' that, according to Spielberg, 'allows a person to take [a] kind of quantum leap and ...go abroad, if you will' (Hodenfield, 1978: 36). When Carlo Rambaldi designed the extraterrestrial figure that communicates with Lacombe via Kodaly hand signals at the end of the film, he based his design of its face on Guffey to form a variant of the Kubrickian 'Star Child' – an amalgam of human child and Roswell 'grey'. Spielberg stated in 1988 that:

Cary Guffey as Barry.

> Ever since *Duel*, I've been looking for a visual narrative – a motion picture story –
> that could be told nearly exclusively through visual metaphors and non-pretentious
> symbolism. (Forsberg: 127)

At the end of the film, as the extraterrestrials appear from the Mothership and Barry
is reunited with Jillian, Spielberg and editor Michael Kahn cut to the four-year old's
face watching the ETs as Jillian takes photographs of them. The juxtaposition of Guffey
and the child-like extraterrestrials cements precisely the kind of visual metaphor that
Spielberg talks about, the idea of 'the child' as a symbol of growth and renewal.

It is perhaps instructive to our understanding of *Close Encounters* that children in
science fiction tend not to be cast as monstrous in the same way that they are in
horror cinema. With 1960's *Village of the Damned* (remade by John Carpenter in
1995) a notable exception, children in science fiction (imbued as they often are
with special powers, or in league with aliens, or aliens themselves) are rarely
vilified; and the child's point of view in science fiction usually engenders hope and
enchantment rather than fear and paranoia. In short, children in science fiction more
often symbolise innocence and potential (*Escape to Witch Mountain* [1975, remake
1995]; *Explorers*, *D.A.R.Y.L* (both 1985), *Flight of the Navigator*, *Aliens* (both 1986)
than corrupted innocence and malignancy (*The Exorcist* [1973], *The Omen* [1976,
remake 2006] *Carrie* [1976, remake 2013]). Even ambiguous representations of
children in science fiction cinema tend to portray their destructiveness as arising

from terrible anger at their mistreatment in an unjust world (*Looper*, [2012], Joe Dante's segment, 'It's a Good Life', in *Twilight Zone – The Movie* (1983), *AI: Artificial Intelligence* [2001]). Since *Empire of the Sun*, Spielberg has become more interested in portraying loss of innocence than the 'celebration of a kind of naiveté' that *Close Encounters* represents (Forsberg, 1988: 129). If we compare *Close Encounters* with Spielberg's more recent science fiction films, *AI: Artificial Intelligence* (2001), *Minority Report* (2002) and *War of the Worlds* (2005), we see that Spielberg's science fiction cinema has become increasingly dark and dystopian. Indeed, *War of the Worlds* is almost a complete inversion of *Close Encounters* in so much as Spielberg presents the genocide of mankind rather mankind's transcendence as the likely outcome of an alien visitation/invasion; and rather than having the protagonist leave behind his family to discover a world beyond the stars as Roy Neary does, Spielberg, in *War of the Worlds*, has Tom Cruise fight tooth and nail to protect his children from the Martians whilst at the same time trying desperately to preserve the innocence of his young daughter (played by Dakota Fanning) as death takes place all around them. A comparison of Barry Guiler (note the significance of his surname) in *Close Encounters* with David, the robot-boy (Haley Joel Osment) in *AI: Artificial Intelligence* shows just how far Spielberg's representation of children has moved from celebrating the innocence of a child, to despairing the naiveté of childhood in a world of genocide and man's inhumanity to man. David's problems are born of his own pre-programmed naiveté in this respect; his inability to grow-up and learn the all-too necessary skills for survival in a cruel world is seen as regrettable. He is ill-prepared for the realities of the world. (The visual metaphor of the little girl in the red coat destined for the funeral pyre in *Schindler's List*, and the Jewish children driven to hide in cess pits in order to survive Auschwitz, marks a pivotal moment in Spielberg's cinema in terms of his changing representation of childhood, portraying a necessary, inevitable, end of innocence.) However, as befitting science fiction tropes, David is not portrayed as malign: his angry obsessive behaviour arises in response to the dystopian world that created him but denies him comfort and belonging. Barry Guiler, by contrast, has a child's receptivity to the benign influence of the extra-terrestrials and this becomes a cause for celebration in *Close Encounters*.

Tom Cruise blindfolds his daughter (Dakota Fanning) to protect her innocence in War of the Worlds *(2005).*

We first see this in his reaction as the toys in his bedroom become animated, activated by the mischievous aliens. He is not frightened (unlike the child whose doll similarly comes alive in the Spielberg-produced *Poltergeist* [1982]) but intrigued by this and goes to investigate the mysterious light that beckons him down the stairs to the kitchen. Spielberg keeps the camera at child-height during the sequence (as he does throughout *E.T.*) emphasising a child's point of view of events; the child's POV is sharply contrasted with that of his mother, Jillian, in the later abduction sequence. In a remarkable moment, Spielberg holds on Guffey's reaction to the unseen aliens which goes through the various stages of surprise, bemusement and finally enchantment. The script notes that 'a game is being played out' between child and alien. (Spielberg teased this extraordinary performance from the four year old by dressing up off-screen actors in animal costumes.)

The theme of a child's receptivity to the unknown influenced Spielberg's casting of the adult roles as well, as he explained:

> I think in casting *Close Encounters* what I was really looking for were actors who were still closer to their own memories of their own childhoods. Richard Dreyfuss was a bigger kid than the children he was raising in his suburban house. François

Truffaut, as he was in life, was a child just of heart. He was just as honest as any man I have ever met in the sense that he was in touch with things that make children eternally optimistic. [The same principle was followed for] everybody in the movie except for some of the more rank and file military personnel [where] I went more for the cynic, the life-hardened adult...we made this picture in the spirit of childhood and believing in things that don't make sense, that only children believe in because it doesn't have to make sense for a child to deeply believe in something. (Bouzereau, 2008)

Distinguishing the 'child-like' from the 'childish' in Spielberg's films is an area that has divided critics. Robin Wood, a detractor of Spielberg in the 1980s, provides a definition of each based on Peter Coveney's study, *The Image of Childhood*, in which the child*like* is aligned with the Romantic vision of Wordsworth and Blake, for whom the child symbolised new growth and regeneration of the self and of civilisation; and the child*ish* is associated with a Victorian sentimentalisation of children, 'the use of the infantile as escape from an adult world perceived as irredeemably corrupt, or at least bewilderingly problematic.' Spielberg in *E.T.*, Wood suggests, seems to hesitate between the two concepts 'before finally committing himself to the childish' (Wood, 2003: 156). Adrian Schober picks up on Wood's conclusion as a simple explanation as to why in *Close Encounters* Roy 'can so easily leave his wife and kids behind for the aliens' in *Close Encounters* (*Senses of Cinema*, 2014). The answer, according to Wood, is that Roy has regressed into infantilism. But Schober then goes further in following Wood's line of thought to question whether Spielberg could be deliberately commenting on the self-limiting narcissistic childishness of the character. Could Spielberg be hesitating in the film between the childish and childlike? Such a reading, Schober concludes, locates ideological contradictions and opposing impulses within Spielberg himself.

We have already established Spielberg's changing views on *Close Encounters*, particularly in terms of Roy's leaving his family behind to board the spaceship, which Spielberg regards nowadays – if not as a regression into infantilism – as an act of irresponsibility that Spielberg does not condone since he has had children of his own. However, speaking in 1978, Spielberg commented revealingly on his own ideology, the childish/child-like in his work and the character of Roy Neary:

I really wanted to take a child's point of view. The uneducated innocence that allows a person to take this kind of quantum leap... and go abroad, if you will. A conscientious, responsible adult human being probably wouldn't. Especially if his life had a lot of equilibrium, he certainly would turn down the chance to go that far abroad. As opposed to someone like Neary, whose whole life sprouted out of model trains... Because, for me, Neary is not so much the father of the family of four, but a member of that family, no different to any of the kids. I think in order to want to go on that journey, you'd have to have that naïve wonderment. He was, for me, in my mind a prime candidate. He was ready even before anything happened to him. (Hodenfield: 36)

If Spielberg hesitates between the child-like and the childish in *Close Encounters*, as Schober suggests, perhaps the reason lies not necessarily in Spielberg's own ideological contradictions as in the simple co-existence of the two states inside Roy. Neary retains a child-like potential, a receptivity to the aliens and what they represent: growth, renewal and willingness to 'go abroad', but at the same time he is kept in a state of *childishness*, not by his own self-limiting narcissism, necessarily, but certainly by social constraint.

J.P. Telotte argues that social authority (government, military, family, workplace) in *Close Encounters* is shown as keeping people in a preternaturally childish state. 'It is that *abnormal* childishness,' Telotte suggests, 'that finally seems so dangerous and incapacitating'. Roy and his wife Ronnie and family are trapped in this incapacitating and unnatural state so that they become, like Ronnie, unable to cope with life's pressures, or, like Roy and the kids, unable to grow up into responsible adulthood. Telotte concludes that 'What is finally needed, the film offers, is a kind of growth and development *through* the innocent and open vision of a child'. Neary undergoes this radical transformation in the course of his encounters with aliens (2001: 152, original emphases).

Roy

In the 1977 *Theatrical* version, Spielberg segues from a shot of the remote farmhouse and Barry running off into the woods to play with his new friends, into Roy's introduction: we see a locomotive in an elaborate toy train set speeding past a model station and level crossing towards a drawbridge, which rises at exactly the wrong time so that the locomotive is derailed. Cut to a close up of Roy's frustrated, sullen face. Here Spielberg juxtaposes the child-like Barry with the childish Roy, but in between the scenes – as a thematic link – Spielberg inserts a shot of a Pinocchio figurine music box playing 'When You Wish Upon a Star'. The song, as we know, symbolises for Spielberg 'stars, magic', the wonder of the cosmos. For Roy, it means a transformation to a child-like state where magic and wonder – the kind that Barry experiences – can again be felt: a seemingly impossible dream (until he has his first encounter). Spielberg returns only once to the figurine later in the film, as if a reminder to Roy of that lost dream as he takes down news clippings and UFO paraphernalia, trying to rid himself of his bizarre obsession and assume the mantle of responsible adult once more. The inclusion of Pinocchio and the song in *Close Encounters* has been interpreted in a variety of ways. Spielberg had originally planned to end the film with the song in its entirety, but changed his mind after previews:

> [T]he audience wanted to be transported into another world along with Richard Dreyfuss as he walked aboard the Mothership. They didn't want to be told the film was fantasy, and this song seemed to belie some of the authenticity and to bespeak fantasy and fairy tale. And I didn't want *Close Encounters* to end just as a dream. (Royal, 1982: 97)

It is easy to see why, for example, the inclusion of Pinocchio and the song has been interpreted as an indication of Roy's yearning for escape into infantilism, and possibly contributes to a reading of the film as 'hymn to regression and emotional retardation'. Perhaps it was for this reason that when Spielberg prepared the *Special Edition* in 1980 he restored the longer, substantially different family scene that he had originally scripted and shot. In this extended version of the scene, Roy is first seen immersed in his model train set and neglecting his son, Brad, who seeks help with his maths homework. When Roy does finally help Brad, he is grudging and sarcastic towards the boy, an indication of the resentment he feels towards his family and his sense of being trapped in his role as suburban dad. His claustrophobia is

Roy and his son Brad, in a scene cut from the 1977 Theatrical *release but reinstated in the* Special Edition *and the* Director's Cut.

shared by his wife, Ronnie, who complains about Roy's clutter; she is clearly desperate to get out of the house and do something as a family, and in turn, resents Roy because he habitually withdraws into his childish hobbies. Indeed all of the family members, including the two youngest children Sylvia and Toby, seem bored and fractious. Toby, in particular, vents his frustration on his sister's dolls, violent action given centre stage by Spielberg as if externalising the underlying tension in the family that threatens to explode into aggression. The scene does not give the sense that this tension arises from *within* the family: this is not a dysfunctional family as such. Rather, each member is suffering in his or her own way from a malaise that seems to be brought on by a lack of stimulation and fulfilment; an absence of what the psychologist Abraham Maslow would term 'self-actualisation'. What this longer scene brings, crucially, is the understanding that the *whole family* suffers from this malaise, not just Roy.

Why did Spielberg cut this scene for the theatrical version? One possible reason is that the scene surely does not encourage sympathy for Roy (Ronnie either, for that matter). It gives us an understanding of why he retreats into childishness, but we don't *like* him for it. In her much reviled dish-the-dirt memoir *You'll Never Eat Lunch in This Town Again*, producer Julia Philips claims that Spielberg panicked after the success of *Star Wars*, which he feared would steal his film's thunder, and subsequently scrapped family scenes and shot more special effects. Certainly Spielberg would have been under intense pressure to produce a commercial hit, and this may have influenced his choice to remove material that would cast his protagonist in an unsympathetic light. The decision was almost certainly made late in the day, as the insert of the Pinocchio figurine needed as a transition between scenes, as we know from Bob Balaban's diary, was one of the extra pieces of filming that led to the opening of *Close Encounters* being delayed at the end of 1977.

It may be that Spielberg was never happy with this particular scene. It is one of the most rewritten and revised in *Close Encounters*, and there is the sense that Spielberg was never able to 'nail' it to his satisfaction. Even the shooting draft of the screenplay differs to what was actually filmed: in the script Roy takes much more of an interest in helping Brad with his maths, and is more sympathetic as a result, as is Ronnie, who is shown entering the room with her eyes closed, complaining in a whimsical way that she feels like 'Toby's hamster' on his wheel.

Ronnie

Spielberg has been much criticised for his negative portrayal of Ronnie Neary in *Close Encounters*. Andrew M. Gordon describes her as 'the most unsympathetic wife in Spielberg's films...criticising, belittling, manipulating and sulking...conventional and closed minded...over concerned with what the neighbours will think and unsympathetic to her husband's nervous breakdown' (2008: 63-64). By 1990, even Spielberg himself regretted the way Ronnie is portrayed in the film:

> I was young, naïve and chauvinistic... She was the bad guy in the movie in a sense. She's not really a bad guy, she's somebody who's trying to preserve her family and save her family from a kind of insanity she's assuming Dreyfuss is experiencing, and doesn't want her family to be tainted by this. (McBride, 1997: 283)

If these criticisms of misogyny are indeed valid, it is an indictment not just of *Close Encounters* but, sadly, of 70s American cinema in general; an era of profound ambivalence towards women on the screen. As Molly Haskell has remarked, 70s American cinema was for women the story of an absence; where 'grown-up women

Spielberg confers with Teri Garr during filming.

were rare as fireflies in January'. Good roles for women were not only scarce, according to Haskell, 'women virtually disappeared from the screen, as sex objects or anything else'; even New Hollywood directors 'burrowed into male-centred violent melodrama' in which women were generally excluded (1987: 372). Melinda Dillon accepted the role of Jillian Guiler only after flipping through the screenplay to the final scene – where Jillian takes the photographs that indisputably prove the existence of extraterrestrials to the rest of mankind – which persuaded her that the character had some importance beyond being just another a dutiful mother protecting her son (not surprisingly, perhaps, Jillian was originally written as a male character). Even so, as a number of critics have noted, Jillian is denied the opportunity to board the Mothership herself. Haskell observes that virtually no American films in the 1970s depict the special qualities of relationships between women on a day-to-day working, or living, basis; and that is certainly true of *Close Encounters* (and Spielberg's films generally – with the exception perhaps of *The Color Purple* [1986]). The film would not even pass the Bechdal Test: Jillian and Ronnie barely get to share a scene together, let alone talk about something else besides a man.

The shooting script actually does give Ronnie some lines of dialogue to articulate her feelings of frustration at her situation, and her character is shown to possess a wit and tenderness largely missing in the film. 'If there are seven days in the week and your mother is at home for all seven of them, how many days are left to your mother?' she asks Brad to work out on his calculator, before announcing plaintively, 'Jesus, can't we do something? I'm serving time in this house.' As she passes the phone to Roy in the script, she 'snuggles up to Roy kissing his ear.' In the shooting script, all the characters seem to bear their frustrations with good humour, which makes for a more sympathetic portrayal of the characters, but perhaps blunts the essential point of the scene; what is missing is the sense of desperation in their situation.

Interestingly, the novelisation of *Close Encounters*, attributed to Steven Spielberg, but actually ghost written by the novelist Leslie Waller, offers a *fourth* version, one that presents a more sympathetic portrayal of Ronnie (and Roy) and clearer, if somewhat more blatant, exposition. It makes it obvious that Ronnie feels the same sense of boredom and frustration with her life that Roy does, and that they both crave a transformation:

Neary winced inwardly. 'You're painting a very dull picture,' he said.

'Give me a different brush'.

'Listen, if you think my job with the power company is some kind of glamor life...' Neary trailed off, wondering how angry she really was. Ronnie had the ability to burn out her anger quickly. 'Listen, when you've fixed one burned-out transformer, you've fixed them all.'

Ronnie stared blankly at him. 'I think it's that new thing they're always talking about,' she said.

'What new thing?'

'Life-style. I think we have to change ours.'

'That's for rich people, honey,' Roy said. 'They just call up the store and order a whole new life-style.'

'Maybe it isn't life-style,' Maybe it's that other thing the magazines talk about... quality of life.'

'Sounds like a soap opera.'

'There has to be more to life than stalking the supermarket aisles looking for three rolls of paper towels for a dollar.'

Neary was silent for a long moment. She had never butted him about how much he earned, or whether they had enough money to live on or not. He'd always assumed they did okay.

'I got a raise in January,' he began cautiously.

She shook her head. 'Wrong track. I'm not talking about money. I don't mind searching for specials in the store, As long as something special is going on somewhere in my life. And, Roy,' she added, 'you know me. I'm easy.'

'Huh?'

'I'm not asking for a weekend in Acapulco. I mean I'm so starved for something to happen. I'd go bananas if you brought me home a flower. One perfect rose.'

Neary winced again. 'I always forget that.'

'When you crave change the way I do,' Ronnie said. 'You'll settle for anything.' (1978: 27-28)

What is particularly significant about the scene as written in the novelisation is that Roy and Ronnie are shown as capable of communicating with each other, and that Ronnie (and the family's) frustrations are not directed so much at Roy's selfish neglect (as they seem to be in the *Special Edition* and *Collector's Edition* versions) as the sense of *ennui* arising from their limiting lifestyle.

Another reason, however, for Ronnie becoming less sympathetic in the film may be Teri Garr's own antipathy towards the character. When she was approached by Spielberg (who had been impressed by her quirky comic timing in a coffee advert; she had also played a small role in Coppola's *The Conversation* [1974]), Garr had not wanted to play Ronnie, a woman whose suburban lifestyle was far from her own experience, and had preferred the role of Jillian (Morton, 2007: 131). Spielberg persuaded her to take the part, however, and she threw herself into method-style research for it. Here Garr describes how she prepared herself to play Ronnie:

I had so many girlfriends at the time and relatives in my family that were married to men and then they just lived their lives through them and they had a bunch of kids and they ran the house and they did all that stuff. ...I wrote so many things about this character, what she did, the work she did all day, what she thought of the neighbours, what she wore, and what shoes she wore... I drove myself down to the mall, and pretended to shop for furniture. I went to have the guy try to sell me a refrigerator or some furniture or a stove. 'Tell me what's good about *this* stove. Tell what's good about *that* stove'. And I got to be like Ronnie Neary. That's the kind of stuff *she* would do – just picking apart these little details, as if they were important. That's the kind of person that Rick Dreyfuss's character was married to. No wonder he was seeing UFOs – she was driving him crazy. (Bouzereau, 1997)

Garr plays Ronnie as a neurotic and controlling, desperate for financial and emotional security, whilst feeling that her world – home, family, domesticity – is constantly under threat of collapse. This leaves little room for the whimsical Ronnie of the screenplay. Garr recalled to Ray Morton that Spielberg's note to her in the casting was that, 'these were middle-class people and the wife was very worried about not being able to make payments on things, so to have my husband go crazy and lose his job would have been terrible' (2007: 132). If Ronnie is conventional and closed minded to the possibility of UFOs, it is quite understandable, given her situation and outlook, and hardly uncommon. Interestingly, Ronnie embodies a quote made by Kubrick to *Playboy* magazine in 1968: 'most people don't really want to think about extraterrestrial beings patrolling our skies and perhaps observing us like bugs on a slide. The thought is too disturbing; it upsets our tidy, soothing, sanitized, suburban Weltanschauung'. This is essentially Ronnie's viewpoint in *Close Encounters*; a survival mechanism perhaps, but one that blinds her to 'what may be the most dramatic and important moment in man's history – contact with another civilisation' (Nordern, 1968: 59).

'Weekend America'

James Kendrick comments that Spielberg's films are constantly torn between 'recognising and celebrating the every-day comforts of Middle-American existence and the sadness, loneliness, isolation, and sense of failure that often hides behind the otherwise serene façade of [suburbia]' (2014: 40). This may well be true in the cases of *E.T.* and *Poltergeist*, but suburbia seems to offer little cause for celebration to the characters of *Close Encounters*. There is no genuine 'community' in the suburbia of *Close Encounters*, for example, despite the neighbours sharing unfenced backyards and holding Sunday brunch block socials. In a scene deleted from all versions, Roy and Ronnie attend one of these neighbourhood get-togethers, where the women gossip in their circle ('ten housewives tired of being married to their houses', the screenplay tells us) and the men make 'Sunday small talk' in theirs. However, when Roy has his break-down later in the film and starts tearing up the backyard for materials with which to build his mountain, those same neighbours stare at him curiously like *he* is the alien, the bug on a slide.

Spielberg has spoken trenchantly about suburbia in his films. In 1978, he talked about the 'insulation of suburban modernisation' in the following terms:

It begins on Sunday: you take your car to be washed. You have to drive it but it's only a block away. And, as the car's being washed, you go next door with the kids and you buy them ice-cream at the Dairy Queen and then you have lunch at the plastic McDonald's with seven zillion hamburgers sold. And then you go off to the games room and you play the quarter games: the Tank and the Pong and Flim-Flam. And by that time you go back and your car's all dry and ready to go and you get into the car and you drive to the Magic Mountain plastic amusement park and you spend the day there eating junk food. Afterwards you drive home, stopping at all the red lights, and the wife is waiting with dinner on. And you have instant potatoes and eggs without cholesterol, because they're artificial – and you sit down and you turn on the television set, which has become the reality as opposed to the fantasy this man has lived with that entire day. And you watch the primetime, which is pabulum and nothing more than watching a night-light. And you see the news at the end of that, which you don't want to listen to because it doesn't conform to the reality you've just been through primetime with. And at the end of all that you go to sleep and you dream about making enough money to support weekend America. (Pirie: 105)

Andrew Britton has taken Spielberg to task for this statement, which he claims is spurious – contradicted by his films in which suburbia is threatened by a 'Power of Evil' (*Jaws*, *Poltergeist*, *Duel*) or visited by a 'Power of Good' (*E.T.*), both of which serve to reassure audiences that 'the world in which one feels trapped and from which one wishes to escape are worth having and fighting for after all' (Britton, 2009: 145) However, in *Close Encounters*, Roy completely rejects the suburban ideal and leaves with the extraterrestrials.

Part of the problem for some critics may be Spielberg's 'loving' recreation of suburbia in the film. Todd Alcott remarks of *Close Encounters*, 'everything is mounted with such great love and understanding of these characters and their world... Spielberg never holds up these suburbanites as ridiculous, he loves these people and wants to capture their world with all the detail he can muster' (July, 2008).

In their preparation for the film Spielberg and Alves referred to Bill Owens' classic 1972 photographic study and social document, *Suburbia*. Owens photographed residents of a Californian suburban community at work and play over a period of a year: he documented family barbeques, Tupperware parties, mothers with their babies, families enjoying leisure time in their car ports and backyards. His photographs depict both the material comforts of white middle-class life but also its cultural shallowness and ethnocentrism. Spielberg essentially follows the same non-judgemental, observational approach as Owens in *Close Encounters*. However, he is also careful to show the pervasive influence of American mass culture and consumerism on suburban lifestyles. As Gordon points out, television sets are always turned on, even if no-one in the house is actually watching them. Spielberg uses real TV programmes – *Days of Our Lives*, *Police Woman* and *Road Runner* cartoons to create 'some kind of reality', one shaped by television (Crawley, 1983: 40). Similarly, well-known 'family' brands – McDonalds, Baskin-Robbins, Budweiser – are placed in scenes to help create a familiar, recognisable but artificial social landscape. It all goes towards presenting what Spielberg has described as the 'anaesthetic of suburbia', a protection from real life. (Sragow, 1982: 111). In the final analysis, we can perhaps see, then, Spielberg's use of suburbia in *Close Encounters* as a visual metaphor for complacency, akin to Kubrick's depiction of a technocratic society in *2001*; for what J. Allen Hynek describes in *The UFO Experience* as 'cosmic provincialism' (1972: 288).

'Weekend America': Spielberg's portrait of suburbia in Close Encounters.

'In America, how can UFOs exist over the sky when *Phyllis and Maud* and *All in the Family* are on television at the same time?' Spielberg commented in 1977, 'When do people go outside and look up any more?' (Combs: 32)

Significantly, when the extraterrestrials knock out the power grid over Muncie, Indiana, amongst those to experience lights-out are McDonald's and a Shell gas station: the UFOs symbolically shut 'weekend America' down – at least temporarily.

Rank and File Roy

A scene featured in the 1977 theatrical version that Spielberg cut from subsequent versions shows Roy at his workplace at the Indianapolis Department of Water and Power. He is given sudden unexpected responsibility when the power goes mysteriously dead across the Indianapolis grid. Neary is sent out to investigate reports of vandalism on the lines. The scene is essentially expository: it explains why Neary would be alone on a deserted highway in the middle of the night where he has a close encounter. Spielberg adds urgency to it by having an argument taking place between two foremen, one of whom gives Neary the job as he knows the technical specifications in that particular area of the grid. Relatively unimportant though the scene may be, it again emphasises the effect of the UFO phenomenon on the rank and file American. Moreover, it shows that at the start of the film Roy is part of that rank and file: Roy is nervous around his superiors and also when he has to exercise authority over the linesmen waiting for orders on the road (a scene in the screenplay but cut from all versions of the film).

One of the key themes of *Close Encounters* is the necessity to pursue personal growth and self-actualisation even though that may well mean stepping out of the rank and file and disobeying authority if need be, actions that require great courage and determination. After his close encounter, we begin to see this transformation in Roy. He questions the official air force line on UFOs, and demands the truth; actively practices civil disobedience, ignores military road blocks, escapes quarantine and gate-crashes the top secret first contact with the extraterrestrials. As Telotte points out, we can see in Roy's journey a version of what Joseph Campbell termed the 'monomyth', an archetypal timeless story that relates a hero's call to action, his initial reluctance to take that call, and his eventual move into a strange, unfamiliar territory where he accomplishes great deeds and returns a hero, bringing back a boon for his people (2001: 105-106). Roy's reward for this is to be given the ultimate responsibility of intergalactic ambassador when he enters the Mothership. Along the way, as Susan Mackay-Kallis observes, Roy has to face powerful psychological and emotional obstacles as well: his family's disbelief and lack of support concerning his close encounter, his fear of going mad, his apprehension about another encounter with the aliens and what that may entail, and his feeling of 'smallness' as the average everyday Joe trying to find the answer to something he doesn't understand. By the end of the film, however, Roy 'has finally found his place and will be "at home" in the universe in a way he never was on Earth' (2001: 166-173).

> 'A close encounter could happen to anyone. It could happen to you. It *does* happen to Roy Neary' (1977 Trailer)

The casting of Richard Dreyfuss as Roy helped Spielberg to solidify his screenplay for *Close Encounters*, and also helped him shape the film's philosophy. Dreyfuss had followed the development of the project since *Jaws*, and lobbied Spielberg tirelessly for the part. According to Dreyfuss, Spielberg finally gave in when he told the director that he needed for the role 'someone who could be a child and yet a man' (Bouzereau, 1997). As Roy, Dreyfuss is quirky, funny, indignant and stoical. He swings from euphoria to despair; and he is not afraid to take us into the darkness of Roy's

Richard Dreyfuss as Roy Neary.

obsessive-compulsion, creating empathy between audience and character.

Early in his career, Dreyfuss became known for playing cocky but amiable characters: Curt, the college kid who becomes obsessed with a mysterious blonde woman driving a 1956 Ford Thunderbird in *American Graffiti* (1973); Duddy, the Jewish hustler who is desperate to acquire land, power and money at any cost in *The Apprenticeship of Duddy Kravitz* (1974); Elliot, the struggling actor who falls in love with a single mother in *The Goodbye Girl* (1977) (shot just after *Close Encounters* and for which he won an Oscar). Later on, he played older, wiser variations but still showing his 'uncanny ability to make annoyingly vain, pompous, whiny or supercilious characters seem both heroic and likeable' (*Richard Dreyfuss Biography*, *Turner Classic Movies*) in *Stakeout* (1987), *Always* (1989), *Mr Holland's Opus* (1995). In *Inserts* (1975), *The Big Fix* (1978) and *Whose Life is It Anyway?* (1981), he plays the underdog fighting for his dignity; another obvious quality he brings to Roy.

Spielberg had originally envisaged the character as an older man, and given him the name of Norman Greenhouse. He offered the part to Steve McQueen, a very different actor, but one whose star persona had stemmed from playing outsiders who also reject the rank and file. When McQueen turned the role down, Spielberg reconsidered Dreyfuss, whose box-office standing had increased massively after *Jaws*, and he revised the script, making Greenhouse a younger man and changing his name to Neary. Jerry Belson was hired, at this point, to work on the screenplay with Spielberg, and they concentrated particularly on the family scenes, fleshing out the humour and the pathos in the relationships (Morton, 2007: 134). Belson was a comedy writer in television partnered with Garry Marshall on shows like *The Odd Couple* (1970-1975). He also wrote the screenplay to Michael Ritchie's *Smile*, and later collaborated with Spielberg and Dreyfuss again on *Always* (1989). Dreyfuss is also likely to have been involved in the rewrite of *Close Encounters*, contributing ideas to Spielberg and Belson, and later to Spielberg, Hal Barwood and Matthew Robbins, who wrote the shooting draft of the screenplay dated May 1976. Many of the humorous touches are in the screenplay; others developed during shooting, improvised by Spielberg, Dreyfuss and the rest of the cast.

The 1977 trailer emphasises the everyman aspects of Roy Neary, who is clearly positioned as the audience-identification figure. A close encounter could happen to anyone, we are told, even us. In the film 'it happens to Roy Neary' and we identify with him because of it. Already noted is Spielberg's tendency – derived from Hitchcock – towards subjective cinema. We are invited through shot/reverse shot and camera movement to *be* the characters. Perhaps Spielberg's greatest example of this takes place in the Kintner boy scene of *Jaws*, which, through careful use of camera positioning, shot/reverse shot, screen wipes and sound mixing, presents the shark attack on the small boy from the point of view of Chief Brody, thereby cementing our identification with the Roy Scheider character. Spielberg uses the techniques of cinema to heightened effect, so that we share Brody's feelings as events unfold. We might call such a sequence as this a 'scene of empathy' (Plantinga 1999: 239-255).

A comparable scene in *Close Encounters* is Roy's encounter with the UFO on a deserted highway. That Roy experiences the encounter alone, with only we, the audience, to share it with him, ties us to him early in the film.

'Help – I'm Lost!'

Spielberg and Dreyfuss immediately establish a humorous tone that contrasts and heightens the tension of the encounter itself. Neary pulls up in his truck in the middle of the road to consult his map. He doesn't know where he is. Another car's headlights appear behind him through the rear windscreen and he waves the car past. A man and woman (perhaps a sly in-joke reference to the couple on the road in *Firelight*) pull past Neary, and the man calls him a 'jackass'. Neary comically trades insults with the man, shouting 'turkey' in response. The moment is a set-up for the film's greatest comic gag: Neary pulls up again at a railroad crossing to consult his map and another set of car headlights appear, like the first, in the windscreen behind him. Neary again waves them to go around, and they instead *rise up* over the truck, unnoticed by Neary who is engrossed in his map reading. At this point in the sequence the audience is ahead of Neary, and this lends dramatic irony to the scene. Neary grabs his torch to investigate the violent rattling of a mailbox. The torch suddenly dies, and then Roy has his encounter, which, as we have seen was closely based on actual encounters reported by J. Allen Hynek in *The UFO Experience*. As in the reports, Roy experiences weightlessness, and his reaction is again comical. Not only in this scene but in the sequences that follow, up to the point where Roy is fired from his job at the DWP the next morning, Roy is made the butt of jokes, and this, too, helps to create a strong sense of empathy with the underdog character struggling to maintain his dignity after the unwanted UFO experience.

As the prolonged encounter goes on, however, we start to see Neary's fear. The camera dollies into him, the first of many such camera movements in *Close Encounters* that act as a magnifying glass on the character's emotional state, subtly suggesting an affinity with that person (even extras are afforded this empathy). Three such camera movements occur in the scene, all with the purpose of bonding us to Roy. The second takes place after the blinding light from the UFO suddenly goes out and Roy is left sitting motionless in his truck, in a state of shock. The camera pushes into him slowly this time, framing him through the side window; gradually he rouses himself to look through the windscreen at the hulking dark underbelly of the spaceship as it passes over the truck. The spacecraft beams its spot light further down the road. The camera holds on Roy's numb reaction – what just happened? His torch comes on – Roy screams – another laugh from the audience. And again as the truck starts; Spielberg is releasing tension as things return to normal. As Roy listens to a report of the spacecraft on the police scanner, the camera dollies into his face again very slowly. We get sense of his fear slowly turning into excitement, as he decides to give chase to the UFOs.

Through wry humour, Spielberg emphasises how absurd the close encounter really is. 'This is nuts!' Roy exclaims on Crescendo Summit after the UFOs whizz past himself, Jillian and Barry, with the police in hot pursuit. We can only share this conclusion. Spielberg piles on the absurdities in the sequences that follow: the sleeping tollbooth attendant who misses the UFOs as they fly past but shouts angrily after the police and Roy as they give chase; the police car that crashes through the guardrail in its eagerness to follow the UFOs over a cliff; Roy's sense of exhilaration from the chase; his loss for words ('It was a red whoosh!') when he tries to explain what he saw to his sleeping wife (who thinks he is rousing her for sex, and tells him 'not now'); the kids comically splayed out in their beds when Roy goes to wake them with the promise, 'it's better than goofy golf!'; Mrs Harris, the neighbour bemused by family's middle-of- the night outing. The comic moments go on and on.

The lightness of touch in these scenes helps make them real. The humour continues fully through this section of the film as Roy returns with his family to Crescendo Summit hoping for a repeat performance of the earlier encounter, but is frustrated when the UFOs fail to comply. Neary's kids exact a revenge of sorts next morning as they paddle his ass with a table-tennis bat while he brushes his teeth – a Spielberg 'human' moment that was scripted, as was the business with Ronnie and the shaving cream, the classic pie-in-the-face gag that shows Dreyfuss at his most clownish.

But *Close Encounters* is a film of light and darkness. As soon as Spielberg has bonded us with Neary through nervous laughter, he abruptly changes the tone. Roy receives news that he has been fired – the seeds of Roy's obsession and later breakdown are sown (in another bit cut from the *Special Edition* and *Collector's Edition*, he is more interested in the mountain shape made by the pillow in his bedroom); and, worse, we see it through the eyes of his kids who sense that the fun is over.

Douglas Trumbull and Immersive Cinema

Criticisms of Spielberg traditionally focus on his tendency to manipulate emotion, making the audience feel rather than think. His critics maintain that Spielberg's is a cinema of sensation rather than intellect. Certainly, intensity and variety of emotion is integral to *Close Encounters*: emotions contained in this film may not be as complex as in Spielberg's later films (or the films of other directors), but there is a depth of feeling in its contemplation of the sublime; through immersion in the narrative and empathy with the characters audiences are invited to feel emotions that they do not feel in the daily course of their lives – the wonder and awe at the cosmos that is intrinsic to the film's message.

There is, on the other hand, of course, the nagging question of spectacle (empty or otherwise, but more often than not, empty), and its continuing dominance in Hollywood. Science fiction cinema, in particular, is a modern 'cinema of attractions' that relies as much, if not more, on special effects than on narrative to draw audiences into the film experience (the intention of most blockbusters being to give the audience nothing more than an entertaining but instantly forgettable ride). It could be argued, however, that the key science fiction directors – Kubrick, Spielberg, Ridley Scott, James Cameron, George Lucas – have used cinema technology as part of their attempt to immerse the viewer *in* the narrative, to take them deeper into the story, the characters and their diegetic world. We might include Douglas Trumbull in this group of filmmakers. Although he is best known for his pioneering special effects in such films as *2001*, *The Andromeda Strain* (1970), *Silent Running* (which he also directed and co-wrote in 1972), *Star Trek – The Movie* (1979) and *Blade Runner* (1982), he has spent much of his career on a technological quest for immersive cinema:

> It is the concept of exploring new cinematic form that has drawn me ever closer to reaching my holy grail of a movie that offers a profound and immersive, overwhelming personal experience. Not an experience empathizing with actors via a third-person voyeurism, but a direct first-person experience where each audience member feels that they are inside the movie – participating IN the movie, not just looking AT the movie. (Trumbull, 2012)

In that quest, Trumbull has known much disappointment at the hands of the studios, which have generally been reluctant to place their trust – and money – in his technological innovations: these have included virtual set systems, 4D simulators, and alternative large screen formats – such as his ill-fated Showscan process. By all accounts, Showscan provided a truly immersive cinema experience. The process, by which 70mm was filmed and projected at 60 rather than 24 frames per second was described by Trumbull as creating in the viewer a profound sense of a window onto reality, 'the surface of the screen disappears. It becomes completely fluid' (Morton, 2007: 123). However, despite its immersive qualities the system did not gain traction with an industry averse to expensive technological upgrades, and also failed to compete with IMAX as a 'luxury' format. This led to Trumbull turning his back on Hollywood after coming into conflict with MGM bosses during the filming of *Brainstorm* (1983), his second and latest feature film to date as director (and which he had originally developed to launch Showscan).

Trumbull has a habit of telling studios what they perhaps don't want to hear. In 2014 he unveiled an experimental science fiction adventure short film called *UFOTOG*, designed to showcase a new process called MAGI (4K 3D at 120 frames per second) that, according to Trumbull, offers audiences a powerful sense of immersion and impact not possible using conventional 24 frames per second or 3D standards. Combined with shooting in virtual environments, Trumbull claims that MAGI 'can explore and discover a new landscape of audience excitement and do it inexpensively and quickly...to make films at a fraction of current blockbuster costs, yet with a much more powerful result on screen' (Trumbull, 2014). However, Trumbull admits that such technological innovations go against present Hollywood thinking which continues to favour huge crews, long shooting schedules and expensive location costs; and it remains to be seen whether MAGI will be embraced by the industry or go the way of Showscan.

Showscan, was, in fact, one of the reasons that Trumbull accepted *Close Encounters*, as Columbia allowed Trumbull to shoot the special effects in 65mm and thereby at the same time equip himself with the 65mm cameras needed to take Showscan forward. Filming the effects in 65mm (duplicating the various separate strips of film onto one final composite negative inevitably results in the degradation of the image which is offset by shooting effects in 65mm) enabled Trumbull to match the effects shots with the rest of the footage which was shot on 35mm anamorphic. For his part, Spielberg had been impressed with Trumbull's work on *2001*, particularly the immersive Stargate sequence which Trumbull had designed and shot using a process he called Slit-scan (based on the work of experimental filmmaker John Whitney – an interesting conjunction of Expanded Cinema and Hollywood FX). Spielberg had already commissioned illustrator George Jensen to storyboard the effects sequences and had worked with Joe Alves on initial designs of the spacecraft. Trumbull's role would be to build the models and determine how they might be integrated into the various shots (Turnock, 2015: 179-200; Morton, 2007: 120-127)

Trumbull partnered with Richard Yuricich and formed a company called Entertainment Effects Group, based in Marina Del Rey, California. Trumbull and his company overtook an entire 13,500 square-foot building, converting it into a complete studio. Installed were rooms for developing, optical printing, and editing; elaborate filming stages with dolly tracks running horizontally and vertically with electronically operated control booths; a wood shop, metal shop, paint shop; and areas for constructing miniature sets, camera and lighting maintenance, and experimentation with techniques and equipment (*Close Encounters* Pressbook, Columbia Pictures, 1977). *Close Encounters* required over 200 effects shots and many of the techniques needed for these were pioneered by Trumbull's group. These included the first use of motion-control using real-time on-location digital recording of camera motion (so that actors and UFOs could be combined in moving camera shots, something not done before *Close Encounters*); Trumbull's group was the first to composite motion-control shots in 65mm. In order to give the UFOs greater mystery and presence on screen Trumbull built a special smoke room inside which to photograph the spaceship models. To create the billowing clouds from within which the UFOs emerge in the film, Trumbull used salt water tanks into which he injected billowing white paint. He also developed a system of 'soft mattes' for retaining the glow of the spacecraft and much-imitated (notably by J.J. Abrams, ad nauseum) lens flare within composite FX shots.

Lens flare has since become a standard technique for making special effects seem 'real', but it is a technique first used in *Close Encounters* and is something for which Spielberg and Trumbull must take the credit. As part of the immersive experience,

Spielberg and Douglas Trumbull.

Spielberg wanted the spacecraft to look like photographically believable objects integral to the mise-en-scène, with the glowing lights of the spaceships striking the camera lens in exactly the same way as a car headlamp would. Such a photographic detail would make the spacecraft seem as real on screen as earthbound objects like trees, mountains, roads. As Spielberg explained:

> I knew what I wanted to put on screen. I had very strong images, maybe I wasn't that good at articulating the images. I'm talking about the nebulous quality of light and how it strikes the optics of a lens and what it does to the lens – it put these kinds of circles around the nodal point to the light. I was describing it that way. I used to park my car on the airport boulevard near LAX and I used to watch all the planes all stacked up out in the sky, all coming in, five miles apart. I thought wouldn't it be amazing if I could get that same effect coming into the final zone at the Devil's Tower in Wyoming. (Bouzereau, 2008)

Lens flare had in fact become a kind of symbol of New Hollywood realism in the early 1970s, as it broke the rules of cinematography of classical Hollywood where such a thing was considered a 'mistake'. The immersive qualities of *Close Encounters* arise in part from its commentary on cinema spectatorship: we watch the characters gaze at UFOs as well as gaze at them ourselves. The UFOs seem to share the same photographic space as the actors. Indeed, the end of the film, when Roy boards the

Mothership, suggests the possibility, as Julie A. Turnock observes, of 'penetrating and *entering the special effect*' (2015: 197). One longs to experience a film such as *Close Encounters* in an immersive format like Showscan in which the surface of the screen disappears and we are left with 'a window on reality'.

Religious Ecstasy, Government Conspiracy and Accusations of Fascism

One of Trumbull's tasks for Spielberg was, according to Turnock, to realise the generalised thematic motif of light in the script, give it material substance and meaning (2014: 194). Numerous critics have commented on Spielberg's quasi-religious use of light in his films: David Bordwell, for example, writes in his blog with Kristin Thompson, *Observations on Film Art*, 'It was in *Close Encounters* that I first noticed his fascination with linking faces and beams of light. In that movie people just watch, transfixed by the luminous aerobatics of the vagrant UFOs and then eventually by the four-alarm light show pumped out by the mother ship' (June 4, 2008). Spielberg has himself referred to his use of 'God Light', which he defines as 'shafts coming out of the sky, or out of a spaceship, or coming through a doorway' (McBride, 1997: 286). The first use of light in *Close Encounters* (and arguably the first in any Spielberg film) that is given explicit religious denotation occurs in Roy's third visit to Crescendo Summit, where he joins other UFO contactees hoping for a second 'visitation'. The scene opens on Roy already watching the sky expectantly as he loads his camera with film, ready to get the indisputable proof he so desperately wants; the confirmation of his belief. The scene's religious overtones survive from Schrader's draft: Roy has returned to his Road to Damascus where the angel of God first appeared to him.

For many of the audience in 1977, *Close Encounters* (like *2001*) was not so much a movie as a religious experience, capable of inspiring a form of religious ecstasy in the viewer. When I first saw the film I responded very strongly to this facet of it; although nowadays, I would connect the appeal of *Close Encounters* to the way it seems to embody aspects of transpersonal psychology, the school of psychology derived from Maslow that believes 'identity or self extends beyond the individual or personal to encompass wider aspects of humankind, life, psyche or cosmos' (Walsh and Vaughan, 1993: 125-182). The film is meaningful in that it offers a glimpse of this self-transcendence, with accompanying emotions that might be *interpreted* as religious ecstasy. In the Crescendo Summit scene, we see this glimmer in the faces not only of Roy and Jillian, but the other contactees on the summit, who gaze with expectation at the approaching lights, hoping for transcendence. Again the camera favours those faces that are child-like, symbolising openness to such an experience. The camera dollies in to a young woman with brown hair; God Light illuminates the faces of an elderly couple. Spielberg does not limit the human potential to his protagonists alone: the whole of mankind shares the capacity for self-transcendence. The John Williams' score emphasises this prospect of Rapture in its use of harp and choir. But we are immediately reminded that socially constructed bounds prevent us from exploring what might lie beyond. The UFOs are in fact government 'black helicopters' sent out for surveillance and – it appears – to psychologically intimidate the UFO contactees. Like the contactees who are forced to flee from the dust and debris blown at them by the choppers, we are unceremoniously brought back down to earth.

It is significant that Spielberg juxtaposes Neary's growing obsession with the Devil's Tower image and the covert government operation to investigate the UFO phenomena. Booker comments that the humans on earth seem to be receiving two entirely sorts of messages from the extraterrestrials:

> On the one hand, there are the innocents and artists (like Roy Neary and Jillian Guiler) who seem to receive intuitive, spiritual calls announcing the alien arrival. On the other hand, the aliens also send mathematical codes to scientists on earth explaining exactly where they would like to meet. (2006: 135)

It is as though the extraterrestrial intelligence understands the social divisions on earth, and that first contact is meant not only for the ruling strata but for all humankind, a necessary step in eliminating divisions. Of course Lacombe is the 'boundary-spanning' character in this respect – as I discuss later in the chapter.

However, *Close Encounters* has been accused of criticising democratic American government whilst actually being in favour of authoritarianism. In his 1977 review for *Variety*, A.D. Murphy commented of the film's denouement at Devil's Tower that

'[I]t's just as well to forget an implicit vibration here that only in a military-scientific-technocratic dictatorship is there order, peace and calm' (Nov 8, 1977). Entman and Seymour felt that the film's theme, structure, and symbolism 'strongly echo those of the films of pre-fascist and Nazi Germany' (1978: 3). Although the film criticises liberal democratic government for trying to hide the truth from the people, its intentions, according to Entman and Seymour, are not radical but neoconservative:

> CLOSE ENCOUNTERS deals with the same failures of democracy. Its solution, of course, is to look beyond earthly politics altogether for a miraculous deliverance. But in the absence of an alien landing, CLOSE ENCOUNTERS instructs people pretty much as neoconservatism does. Don't expect much from government—and don't worry about it because others will arrange things for you. (1978: 6)

How valid an argument is this? Entman and Seymour's reading of the film ultimately hinges on its production context rather than Spielberg's personal politics: *Close Encounters* is a blockbuster and therefore immediately ideologically suspect, especially given the much-publicised problems of Columbia Pictures at the time – a company that was, as the authors note, 'looking desperately to improve its market share' (ibid.). However, if the film offers as a solution to the issue of social alienation, 'the aliens', as Entman and Seymour contend, is the premise of first contact mere escapism? Are the extraterrestrials in *Close Encounters* Messiah figures that will solve our problems for us, or do they represent a more complex notion of post-humanism, the Other within?

The Abduction of Barry

John Landis opines on *Trailers from Hell* that *Close Encounters* contains two truly great sequences: the early scene in the air craft control tower which he praises for its staging and the alien abduction of Barry, a scene that he considers 'truly terrifying'. The abduction scene was added to the screenplay by Hal Barwood and Matthew Robbins fairly late in the day, as a motivation for Jillian Guiler: her son is taken by the aliens and therefore she travels to Devil's Tower in the hope that he will be returned to her there. As a sequence of 'light horror... and sci-fi menace'

(Rowley, *Senses of Cinema*, 2006) it is curiously generic, even intertextual. Previously mentioned is the fact that the scene owes much to Hitchcock's *The Birds*, in which the protagonists barricade a remote house against attack. The décor of the Guiler house – with its drab yellow wallpaper – evokes that of *The Birds*, *Squirm* and *The Exorcist*, all notable horror films that feature similar invasion scenarios inside family homes. Alien abductions taking place at a remote farmhouse would become a staple of UFO movies post-*Close Encounters* – *Communion* (1989), *Lifted* (2006), *The Fourth Kind* (2009) to name just a few; in particular, M. Night Shyamalan would take inspiration from the scene for *Signs* (2002) which draws also on the August 1955 Kelly-Hopkinsville true case in which a family were menaced in their farmhouse by humanoids from a UFO. The scene also seems to explicitly reference *The Searchers*, despite, as previously noted, Spielberg's protests to the contrary. Jillian and Barry are menaced by a red light that shines in at them from outside. In the siege sequence of *The Searchers*, a glowing red sunset shines into the Edwards farmhouse from the open door, symbolising imminent Comanche attack. A cowboy movie is briefly glimpsed on the television in the Guiler house in the midst of attack – it may well be *The Searchers*. Ford's film, after all, concerns abduction by 'alien people', and comments on the Puritan's fear of other races.

Spielberg bookends the sequence with shots of Jillian outside the homestead; as the clouds billow ominously in the darkening sky signalling the imminent arrival of the UFOs, the camera tracks into Barry staring out through the window with joyous excitement. Throughout the sequence Spielberg emphasises the differing reactions of mother and child to the UFO visitation. Barry regards the extraterrestrials as his friends ('they play nice', he informs Jillian in the screenplay). Spielberg tracks the camera into Barry twice – the second time to show his delight at the 'toys' on offer (Spielberg obtained this reaction from Guffey by unwrapping a giftbox containing toys off camera, hence Guffey's spontaneous line in the film).

Jillian, on the other hand, regards the UFOs as a terrifying threat. As Jillian barricades the house against the spacecraft (which are shown only as blinding orange, blue and red lights piercing keyholes, shutters, doors and from inside the fireplace), Spielberg mounts a suspense sequence that slowly builds into full-blown nightmare. This was the scene most bolstered in post-production after editing, showing, from Jillian's point of view, the invading force that she fights to keep out. Spielberg wanted greater intensity in the scene, and added the most terrifying moment afterwards: where Jillian watches in mute horror as the unseen alien force tries to enter by the heating vent in the floor, the screws inexorably undoing themselves in huge close up.

Most of the scene is played with the lights out, in shadow. The scenario becomes akin to that of *Night of the Living Dead* (1968), another farmhouse laid siege to by mysterious assailants. Poltergeist-like phenomena a' la *The Exorcist* and *Carrie* bring the sequence to a climax: the vacuum cleaner starts to move by itself, whizzing past Jillian's feet; 'Chances Are' by Johnny Mathis, with its incongruous lyric, 'Cause I wear a silly grin, the moment you come into view' sounds from the record player; finally the kitchen appliances come alive, glowing in an alien red light. The same red light pierces the louvred windows, bathing Jillian and Barry. It becomes a vision of the inferno, and when Barry is pulled through the dog flap by an unseen force, it is as if he is sucked into hell itself.

Effective though the sequence undoubtedly is in conveying fear of the unknown, on repeated viewings its contrivance becomes apparent, not just in terms of its function in providing Jillian's motivation within the story, but in its playing with our perceptions of the extraterrestrials. Are they friend or foe? Clearly Barry sees them in a different way to how Spielberg wants us to see them as menacing and frightening in the sequence. But it is then difficult for us to reconcile their behaviour in this section of the film and the beatific child-like creatures who finally reveal themselves to us at the end of *Close Encounters*. Co-producer Michael Phillips claims that Spielberg worried during the screenwriting process that his conception of benevolent aliens might not be well-received in an era where Hollywood cinema reflected a general feeling in America of cynicism and despair following Watergate and Vietnam, and even considered changing the script to recast the aliens as hostile. We can see Spielberg therefore electing to keep the extraterrestrials ambiguous in their intentions until the final scene where he ultimately reveals them as friendly. This, however, still raises issues of apparent inconsistency. After all, Jillian, in a previous scene at Crescendo Summit, brought Barry along *hoping* for another close encounter. As M. Keith Booker comments:

The UFOs invade Jillian's house to abduct her son, Barry.

The film does seem determined to make the behaviour of the aliens appear inscrutable, and many of their strategies do not seem to make sense from a human perspective. Among other things, the aliens seem remarkably oblivious to the pain and suffering they might have caused to human beings in their decades-long program of abduction of humans. Nor do they seem concerned about the lives and families (like the Nearys) that might be wrecked by the oddly mysterious nature of their arrival. (2006: 134)

Perhaps the key phrase here, then, is 'do not make sense from a human perspective.' The sequence, when considered with these words in mind, does speak to the essential 'unknowable-ness' of the aliens in *Close Encounters*. Their intelligence and culture may well be unfathomable to human beings, and their motives for contacting us may be impossible to decipher. Communication beyond the most basic greeting may be completely unachievable because of fundamental difference in species intelligence. This, however, seems to be Spielberg's point: perhaps it is simply enough for humans and extraterrestrials to co-exist. Depictions of Otherness in 1980s science fiction cinema have been much criticised (Britton, 2006: 147; Wood, 2003: 158-160; Sobchack 2004: 292-199) for making the aliens too like us (thereby erasing human alienation in the process). *Close Encounters*, however, seems to revel in the strange and the absurd in the meeting between human and extraterrestrial. The capacity, ultimately, for altruism may be the only thing that the human race and extraterrestrials in *Close Encounters* have in common; and Roy Neary (and by extension the rest of humanity) may learn precisely nothing of technological or cultural value aboard a Mothership whose technology and inhabitants are beyond human comprehension. Spielberg may well have been influenced by Kubrick's *Playboy* comments on the early 1970s studies of dolphin intelligence undertaken by Dr. John C. Lilly who, considering the possibility of interspecies communication, wrote of the bottle-nosed dolphin (quoted by Kubrick), 'it is probable that their intelligence is comparable to ours, though in a very strange fashion...They may have a new class of large brain so dissimilar to ours that we cannot within our lifetime possibly understand its mental processes' (Nordern, 1968:57). (Hollywood was much enamoured with Lilly in the 1970s: Mike Nichols loosely based his 1973 science fiction-thriller *The Day of the Dolphin* on Lilly; and Paddy Chayefsky took Lilly's experimentation with psychoactive drugs and sensory deprivation and turned it into the afore-mentioned *Altered States*, directed by Ken Russell in 1980.)

Spielberg seems to suggest that our very failure to understand the aliens in *Close Encounters* may lead to transformation of the self. First contact, according to Kubrick, promises to 'divest man of his smug ethnocentrism and shatter the delusion that he is centre of the universe' (Nordern, 1968: 51). Normal ethics need not apply as we cannot assume that ET will be like us.

Air Force Debunk

Intriguingly, there exists a rarely acknowledged 'UFO discourse' in the script of *Close Encounters* (specifically shooting draft screenplay dated May 1976) that not only challenges nay-saying Spielberg critics but guides us to a clearer understanding of Spielberg's 'preferred reading' of the film. Throughout the screenplay there are a number of explicit references within the dialogue to the messianic role of aliens, Jungian psychoanalysis and authoritarianism. These references are unlikely to be deliberate attempts to ward off ideological criticism (although they go some way towards this) but rather commentary on debates surrounding UFOlogy of the time that seem to direct us to how Spielberg wanted his film to be read. This dialogue has, in all cases, been deleted or modified during the shooting process, as Spielberg refined the scenes with his actors. Much of the deleted dialogue, illuminative as it is, is simply too didactic to work on film: it delivers messages too bluntly. However, in screenplay form it helps to clarify those messages, which in the film, are necessarily left ambiguous or implicit.

The air force debunk scene in which Neary attends a meeting at the DAX Air Force Base hosted a Major Benchley for the UFO contactees was cut in its entirety from the *Special Edition* but reinstated in the *Collector's Edition*. The scene suggests that the air force is actively attempting to cover up the UFO sightings; in the *Theatrical* version it is directly followed by a sequence depicting preparations for the nerve gas hoax that will be used during the evacuation of the Devil's Tower landing site. The juxtaposition harks back to the UFOs and Watergate conspiracy thriller angle that was Spielberg's original approach to the material. The presence of television cameras at the meeting highlights a Spielberg theme developed in *The Sugarland Express*: the outcome of such public events is likely to be determined by the media. Television news is thus the government's ally in controlling public response to the UFOs in *Close Encounters*, and a crucial tool in the evacuation of the landing zone as we see later in the film. Roy is, however, savvy to the presence of the TV cameras turning the issue into a circus. 'You can't fool us by agreeing with us.' He tells Benchley, indicating his suspicion of authority. In the screenplay Spielberg writes of those present at the meeting, 'The country folk were in sharp contrast to the Air Force brass,' (1976: 109). In the script, Neary demonstrates his protest against the obvious air force cover up by rigging the lighting circuits of the building so that the lit and darkened office windows form the letters: U.F.O. In the film, however, Neary's move towards such rebelliousness is more gradual, his character growth is spread through the story.

In the May 1976 screenplay Spielberg uses the air force debunk scene to voice debates about the wisdom of disclosing alien contact to the public; this locates *Close Encounters* within the discussions taking place at the time among scientists – like Carl Sagan – involved in the S.E.T.I. (Search for Extra-Terrestrial Intelligence) concerning an appropriate Post-Detection Policy to be implemented by governments following the discovery of extraterrestrial life. Should the public be told, or is public disclosure likely to cause a massive traumatic cultural shock in the population? In the screenplay, Spielberg has a character named 'Reasonable Man' question Major Benchley outright:

Airforce officials debunk UFO sightings in a public meeting with contactees. A scene cut from the Special Edition.

> Do your people feel the human race is not prepared to live with the cultural impact that the truth could have on mankind?

Benchley replies in such a way as to present the counter-argument:

> If indeed this were true, I'm certain we could live with it. We live in the shadow of atomic annihilate (sic) in nine minutes.

Later in the scene (in the screenplay but not the film) another 'audience aside' character delivers a speech that in many ways debunks the Messiah reading that critics have levelled at the film. This character appears in the film as the civilian sitting beside Major Benchley who 'seems to outrank the 'brass'. He is the one who makes the *Fortean Times*-like comment that 'there are all kinds of ideas that it would be fun to believe in: mental telepathy, time travel, immortality, even Santa Claus' (Roberts Blossom, of course, spins a yarn about Big Foot later in the scene as the meeting deteriorates into farce):

> I believe in life elsewhere. The odds are against there not being...but the expectation that we are going to be saved from ourselves by some interstellar intervention works against the necessity <u>for us to solve our own problems</u>.

Spielberg underlines this last phrase in the screenplay as I have here. It is an intriguing direct address to the audience that appears to want to debunk any reading of *Close Encounters* as a film that advocates authoritarianism or an appeal to superhuman agencies as the only solution to the world's problems.

'I Did Not See My Mother's Tits Coming in Low over the Mount Pleasant Foothills'

We sometimes forget that until well into the 1980s (with his adaptations of *The Color Purple* and *Empire of the Sun*), Spielberg was largely dismissed by critics as a 'boy's own' director of fantasy-adventure. Indeed, *Schindler's List* is frequently cited as the start of Spielberg's mature period as an artist. It is difficult to dispute that Spielberg's films since *Schindler's List* have become darker and more troubling, and that an overriding theme has emerged in his mature work of man's inhumanity to man. And yet, in retrospect, many aspects of *Close Encounters* prevent it from being as light-hearted as critics tend to remember it. *Close Encounters* has dark and painful moments of its own, especially in the scenes that portray Roy's UFO obsession and the subsequent the breakdown of his family. James Kendrick, who has devoted a full-length study to the darkness in Spielberg's work, writes compellingly on the ambiguity of the aliens invading the minds of the UFO contactees, that, on the one hand, marks them out as 'the chosen ones' but, on the other, subjects them to emotional torture and obsession, destruction of family life and social ostracism (2014: 52-54). Kendrick suggests that such psychological invasion seems unnecessary given the God-like abilities of the aliens. While Spielberg incorporated true cases of psychological disturbance and family breakdown reported in those who had experienced close encounters, psychic phenomena as featured in *Close Encounters* is not generally thought to be part of the UFO experience.

A number of critics have commented on Spielberg's own family breakdown as a child in the form of his parents' divorce, and the likely effect it had on Spielberg, the artist. *Close Encounters* might be seen, these critics suggest, as a playing out of this childhood trauma by Spielberg through his art and is what led him to return to the film at various stages in his career, re-cutting and refining it. It does seem that Spielberg's energies for the *Special Edition* had been mainly spent rethinking and revising the film's portrait of Neary's emotional collapse and subsequent family breakdown, and this central section of the film has been the one subject to the most significant revisions in both the *Special Edition* and the *Collector's Edition*, suggesting that this may be well have been an aspect of the film that Spielberg found personally uncomfortable. However, *Close Encounters* can also be seen to reject psychoanalytical readings of Roy's obsession with UFOs in favour of cosmic ones.

The implanted image/obsession motif was, according to Morton, the idea of writer/ director Brian De Palma and dates back to 1974 when the story was being developed by Spielberg and Paul Schrader (2007: 65). De Palma, of course, explored psi phenomena in *Carrie* and *The Fury* (1978); and directed the psychological thriller *Obsession* (1976, also scripted by Schrader), inspired by Hitchcock's masterpiece about destructive male fixation, *Vertigo* (1958). The public fascination with ESP in the 1970s coincided with the emergence of New Age thinking and the popularity of the Human Potential Movement whose beliefs centre on the concept that untapped psychic potential exists in all of us. The Human Potential Movement, in particular, was strongly influenced by Maslow's theory of self-actualisation as the supreme expression of human life. Psi power (usually in the forms of telepathy, telekinesis and/or mind control) is, of course, a staple of science fiction cinema, with *Scanners* (1981), *The Sender* (1982), *The Dead Zone* (1983), *Firestarter* (1984), *Jumper* (2008), *Gamer* (2009) and *Looper* (2012) amongst the more notable examples.

As a plot motif the implanted image in *Close Encounters* is certainly essential in that it provides the means by which the UFO contactees know where geographically first contact is to take place. Spielberg was concerned to make sure that Roy's obsession with the mountain shape was clear to audiences, and, after previewing the film to the public in October 1977, reshot a segment of the third Crescendo Summit meeting where Roy tells Jillian that since their close encounter he has been seeing the mountain shape in 'shaving cream, pillows...This means something, this is important.' Psychologically the implanted image may be considered necessary too, if one allows that *Close Encounters* entertains the Jungian notion that UFOs may be part of the collective unconsciousness, manifested as psychic projections. In some ways though, *Close Encounters* seems to follow more closely than it does Jung, the ideas of the sociologist and UFO researcher Jacques Vallee (whom Spielberg consulted prior to production, and on whom it is often said the Claude Lacombe character is based). In his book *The Invisible College* Vallee suggests that UFOs may not be extraterrestrial spacecraft but manifestations of a 'different level of existence, a reality that seems to cut through our own at right angles.' He claims, 'I believe that a powerful force has influenced the human race in the past, and is influencing it again' (1975: 6). But so far unresolved for Vallee is the question of whether such a force originates entirely within human consciousness, or is the result of alien intervention. 'The whole nature of the UFO phenomenon is ambiguous', Colin Wilson concluded of Vallee's ideas in 1978, 'but the steady build-up of UFO sightings is causing a shift in human consciousness, a new attitude towards the universe' (1978: 563).

Critics have, however, continued to read psychoanalytical meanings into *Close Encounters*. Andrew M. Gordon posits such a reading with reference to the work of psychoanalyst, Christopher Bollas (*The Shadow of the Object: Psychoanalysis of the Unknown Thought*, New York University Press, 1987):

> Bollas speaks of 'the transformational object', a memory from early object relations, where the mother 'continually transforms the infant's internal and external environment.' In later life we may 'search for an object that is identified with the metamorphosis of the self'. In aesthetic experiences, for example, we may feel an uncanny fusion with an object, 'something never cognitively but existentially known'. Bollas claims this is a recollection of the fusion with the maternal 'transformational object'.

> Many adults search frantically for total transformation which they imagine will come about through religious or ideological experience. This obsessive craving can be understood as 'a kind of psychic prayer for the arrival of the transformational object: a secular second coming of an object relation experienced in the earliest period of life'.

> Roy Neary's obsessive search can be considered a quest for the transformational object, a pilgrimage that goes backwards from adulthood to infancy. (Gordon, 2008: 60)

Gordon cites Bollas's notion of the transformational object in support of his reading of *Close Encounters* as an allegory of regression to a primitive or pre-oedipal stage.

The UFOs are Roy's transformational object, and by extension, the film itself functions as ours. Roy's and our desire for total transformation stems from our early infant pre-memory of fusion with the maternal 'transformational object'. It is certainly an interesting reading of the film if one wishes to place a psychoanalytical meaning on the film over and above the cosmic one.

In the shooting draft screenplay dated May 1976, Spielberg includes another pointed 'audience aside' that references 'Isakower's phenomenon' in connection with Roy's obsession with the mountain shape. On the way to the Dax Air Force Base for the meeting with Major Benchley, Ronnie tells Roy that she has read about the phenomenon in Cosmopolitan:

> RONNIE
>
> The fact that these things came closer and closer represents your mother's breast with its promise of food. When satisfied, you the infant, lose interest in the breast which goes away, getting smaller and smaller. The shape of the female breast is...

Ronnie is clearly trying to convince Roy that what he is experiencing has a psychological explanation. However, Roy brusquely responds:

> ROY
>
> Ronnie, I did not see my mother's tits coming in low over the Mount Pleasant foothills.

We might read this brief exchange as teasing the audience with a psychological meaning for Roy's mysterious *Close Encounter*. Or perhaps it is meant to refute such a mundane rationalisation of the UFO phenomenon. However, later in the May 1976 screenplay, in a moment probably never filmed (but retained in the novelisation as below), Roy fixates on Ronnie's breasts which remind him of the vision implanted in his mind by aliens:

> Neary gripped the blouse at her shoulders and pulled. It ripped and the tattered ends pinned Ronnie's arms to her sides. He pulled the brassiere straps off her shoulders and slid the thing down to her stomach, and then he slid down to her breasts and...fixated. Almost immediately the anxiety flowed out of him.

Perhaps these moments were omitted from the film as their irony did not sit well with the rest of the film: this moment of breast fixation was to end the scene (deleted from the 1997 *Theatrical* version but reinstated in the *Special Edition* and the *Collector's Edition*) where Roy locks himself in the bathroom and Ronnie breaks in to find him fully clothed in the shower. Tonally, it would have made an already disturbing scene even more troubling. Spielberg already had his doubts about the scene even without the breast fixation, deeming it, 'almost another movie' (Shay, 1978: 72).

Awe and Revelation

Freudian readings of *Close Encounters* have interpreted Roy's obsessive sculpting of a 'giant excremental totem phallus' (Wood, 2003: 158; Britton, 2009: 151) as evidence of his regression to infantilism. Telotte, on the other hand, sees this regression as a necessary stage in his evolution from a preternaturally childish state towards a new found maturity and sense of purpose, 'a journey that represents humanity's own growth into something like cosmic adulthood' (2001: 153). In Maslow's terms, Roy journey is one to self-actualisation, even self-transcendence. Seen this way Roy's building the mountain in his den is part of this self-actualisation, a gradual realisation of his inner potential that leads in turn to greater self-revelation. As Spielberg told *Rolling Stone* in 1978:

> I used the Van Gogh analogy to Richard many times when I justified the psychotic behaviour in building the mountain in the den. I used the Van Gogh madness parallels several times. A person who is an artist – and Neary is an artist, probably all the people who wound up there are artists of some sort, even if they had no external ability, they certainly had something inside of them that made then worthy. (Hodenfield, 1978: 36)

Key to Neary's self-actualisation, then, is a willingness to release that thing inside of him that makes him worthy, but has been hitherto repressed. Like Jillian and the others, artistic expression in sculpting, painting, or whatever form, has taken a back seat in their lives which have been governed instead by child-rearing, low level employment, and (as written in the screenplay) 'the tasteless puree of terrestrial pabulum' that makes up their daily lives. Reward, however, for responding to the call of the cosmos through artistic expression, is revelation of meaning. Spielberg deliberates holds back from revealing too much, however, making the sense of revelation gradual; but by doing so, that sense of revelation becomes greater, more powerful and awe-inspiring as the film goes on.

Revelation, for Neary, comes in three stages. The first when he attempts to dismantle the small clay mountain sculpture in his den. He only succeeds in sheering off the top, but this reveals to him for the first time the shape that is 'right', something that has eluded him up to now and only fuelled his obsession with the mountain shape even more (most memorably in his sculpting the mashed potato on his dinner plate). Of course the sometimes obsessive need to get it right – to make the reality conform to the idealised image held in the mind – is a trait of all artists. Spielberg deliberately underplays the scene of revelation, keeping it intimate: tight medium shot of Dreyfuss as he moves towards the sculpture. Cut to his point of view, as the camera moves into a close up of flattened top of the mountain. Back to Dreyfuss as he moves closer to the camera, beads of sweat becoming visible on his forehead. No music, only the diegetic sound from the television counterpointing the moment with irony – sound effects from the Chuck Jones/Warner Bros cartoon *Duck Dodgers in the 24th and a Half Century* (1953), itself a parody of the science fiction cinema of its time.

The second revelation for Neary is also ironic and underplayed. After filling the house with dirt and rubbish, Roy is shown to have built a huge version of the mysterious mountain shape in his den. Although he has followed his instincts in doing so, he is at first none the wiser as to the meaning of the shape. Spielberg presents this in another of his long takes, revealing first a dirtied dishevelled Neary – looking very much the mad sculptor – and then his absurd creation, which dominates the room; Spielberg then pulls back the camera to frame a television set – on and playing daytime TV – and a telephone, which Neary uses to call Ronnie. As Neary – spent and depressed and clearly having doubts – tries to convince Ronnie that it was all 'a joke', Spielberg holds on the TV showing a news flash. We, the audience, briefly – almost subliminally – glimpse the mountain shape in the report but Neary doesn't.

Roy and his giant Devil's Tower.

A moment later, the shape reappears on the TV screen; Roy still hasn't seen it, and we, the audience, are then left in terrible suspense , thinking that Roy – who is too busy on the phone, unwilling it seems to let go of his old self – might miss the clues given on the TV and remain 'lost'. Audiences, of course, love this moment of superior positioning, whereby they spot the clues to the mystery ahead of the protagonist and then wait in suspense for the hapless hero to catch up. Spielberg uses graphic matches to take us from Neary's astonished reaction to Jillian's; from the image of the mountain on Roy's TV to the same on Jillian's. Thereby, Roy's reward is two-fold: from isolation to community with the other contactees like Jillian; sharing the moment of revelation with others makes it more meaningful.

Thus the third and greatest moment of revelation happens to both Roy and Jillian as they travel together to the mountain that they have finally been able to identify as Devil's Tower. This moment is perhaps Spielberg at his most inspired, his most intuitive. In the screenplay it is again underplayed. Roy and Jillian are driving together on the Wyoming country road. The car stops dead. We see Roy and Jillian looking through the windscreen. Cut to their point of view: the Devil's Tower peak in the distance. On location, however, Spielberg had a visual idea that immeasurably improved the moment dramatically as Roy and Jillian see the Devil's Tower for the first time in reality. This sudden inspiration seems to have occurred because of the lay-out of the location, although it is possible, perhaps, that a similar moment in *Once Upon A Time in The West* (1968) inspired him. Indeed, the sequences in

Roy and Jillian see Devil's Tower in reality for the first time.

Wyoming see Spielberg and Zsigmond at their most pictorial, making full use of the landscape in a series of breath-taking compositions. Rather than simply cutting from Roy and Jillian looking through the car windscreen, Spielberg has them get out of the car and walk up a small hill. The camera cranes up with them to reveal the awe-inspiring Devil's Tower in the background, a real tangible object sharing the frame with the actors. As Mark Cousins comments:

> This scene...shows Spielberg's filmic signature: the awe and revelation scene. Wide shot, then the camera dollies to people looking at something through a screen. We want to see what they see, but Spielberg doesn't cut to it. Instead, the scene builds. They get out (of the car). We track and rise, and the music rises (2001).

Spielberg has incorporated similar awe and revelation scenes in his subsequent films, albeit rarely as powerfully as this. Partly the power of the scene arises from the fact that Spielberg, as Cousins point out, delays the revelation; rather than cutting straight to it, he makes us wait for it. Partly, of course, John William's score, working in tandem, lends the scene added impact. The camera movement itself has an almost operatic quality, evoking the joy and relief that Roy and Jillian feel at finally seeing the Tower for themselves, a richly deserved vindication after the pain they have suffered. By underplaying previous revelations, Spielberg also heightens the emotional impact of this one. But the scene is uniquely powerful for one other reason: it depicts the point where Roy begins to self-actualise; the moment from which he starts, in Spielberg's words, to 'lose his strings, his wooden joints', to become a real person.

'Who the hell are you people?'

Of Roy's spiritual journey, Telotte writes:

> Breaking free from that old perspective, countering that lost feeling, it seems, is a difficult task, requiring force, an imaginative leap, even a willingness to break the rules. (2001: 155)

Roy's movement towards self-actualisation requires him to break with the rank and file, an action vividly depicted in his capture and subsequent break from detention at the army decontamination camp near the Devil's Tower. Roy, in effect, leads a mutiny of contactees, who are hunted down by the army before they are able to reach the extraterrestrial landing site on 'The Dark Side of the Moon': the hidden plateau on the other side of the mountain. Only Jillian and Roy are able to make it to the other side where their reward is first contact with the extraterrestrials. In effect this sequence of defiance against the army is a test of Roy's mettle, to see if he really is worthy of becoming humanity's representative aboard the Mothership. In a sense, it is his defiance, as much as childlike openness – his courage and willingness to break the rules – that makes him worthy of being 'chosen'.

The interrogation of Neary by Lacombe and Laughlin remains incredibly compelling for this reason. In the novelisation we are told that Neary feels failure, defeat and doubt in the face of military authority. He despairs that 'he'd never learn what the mountain meant'. In the scene, Dreyfuss perfectly captures this as the little man fighting against feelings of intimidation. The despair, however, leads to indignation. Neary, as representative of the rank and file, the 'everyman', becomes the people's champion and spokesperson. Later, amongst the contactees in the army helicopter, waiting to be transported out of the decontamination zone, he proves his faith by removing his gas mask, confirming what he knew only intuitively. Again, only those willing to break the rules and fight for their beliefs make it to the higher ground. We can perhaps see here the origins of *Close Encounters* as an early 1970s countercultural text, akin to the anti-authoritarian *One Flew Over the Cuckoo's Nest* (1975).

Lacombe is, of course, the humanist figure who recognises the struggle between the chosen ones and the establishment; he facilitates the breakout of the contactees, admitting as a government scientist that 'they belong here more than we'. Susan Mackay-Kallis describes Lacombe as a boundary-spanning character (2001: 172). He is a scientist on the one hand, but on the other, he is a man of almost child-like intuition: thereby he acts as mediator between the aliens and the army during first contact, and ultimately facilitates Neary's union with the extraterrestrials at the end of *Close Encounters*. By doing so, he enables Roy to achieve the very highest state of being: that of *self-transcendence* – the transpersonal state by which knowledge is positively correlated, according to Maslow, with a sense of mystery, awe, humility, ultimate ignorance, reverence and a sense of oblation – surrender to the divine (Maslow, 2000: 178).

John Williams

I have purposely left discussion of Williams' contribution to *Close Encounters* until late in the analysis. There are several reasons for this: firstly, the film's soundtrack is traditionally composed and recorded after the film has been edited and the final version 'locked'; the composer therefore is the last contributor in the process of telling the film narrative – he or she becomes, in effect, the final arbiter of the film's meaning. Another reason is that Williams' contribution to *Close Encounters*, whilst adding a great deal to the film, also seems to detract from it in various ways.

Williams is, of course, well-known for his symphonic approach to film music, a return to traditional Hollywood scoring where 'audiences are told exactly what to feel and how to react at every moment', after a period in the 1960s where 'many directors rejected scored music altogether in favour of pop songs, jazz or no music at all' (Boorman, 1985: 219-220). Williams' scores for *Star Wars* and *Close Encounters* have long been seen as a significant factor in their New Hollywood blockbuster status, and as such have been described as 'remarkable for their rhetorical power' (Lerner, 2004:

97). In the case of *Close Encounters*, the Williams score has been said by Neil Lerner (following the argument of Britton, Wood, Entman and Seymour and Tony Williams) to fortify the film's 'authoritarian rhetoric' (ibid: 106).

Whatever one's views on the ideology of *Close Encounters*, it is certainly difficult to dispute Lerner's claim that 'what is so remarkable about Williams' scores – and they are considerable achievements in the history of musical style – is the way that they so effectively limit any oppositional readings of the films that they accompany' (ibid.) There are times, in *Close Encounters*, when the various contradictions in the script seem to be exacerbated by the score. We can see how Spielberg's essentially cosmic message has been muddied at times because of these and through editorial tinkering brought about by the commercial pressures on Spielberg (and, it must be said, his own personal desire) to create a box office hit. Williams' score, in places, leaves little ambiguity as to how the film demands that it be read: as commercial blockbuster cinema. At other times, its romantic sweep threatens to overshadow the film's nuanced depiction of first contact as 'formal, gentle, and a little strange' (Ebert: 1977), blunting the sensibilities of the audience, particularly in the last sequence of the film – as I discuss shortly.

Spielberg with John Williams.

Lerner contends that Williams provides music that 'fits the specification of the director' (2004: 106). This, however, seems to oversimplify the relationship between Spielberg and Williams, described by the director as one he has very little control over:

Once Johnny sits down at the piano, it's his movie, it's his score. It's his original overdraft, a super-imposition. (Tuchman, 1978: 50)

Having said that, there is little doubt that Spielberg attributes the extraordinary commercial success of his films partly to Williams' emotionally powerful music, and is thus quite willing to allow Williams's scores to function as 'a partner in the narrative' (Bouzereau, 1997). Although Williams, in his own words, felt that the music for *Close Encounters* should be 'abstract and impressionistic and otherworldy', the score he composed can be divided into two technical groups: 'One is a kind of romantic area, one side of it, where the notes are recognisable as notes and have tonal harmonies.' (Williams generally uses this approach to emphasise the excitement and human drama of the story.) The second group is 'non-tonal, where there's no tonal relationship from phase to phrase from note to note.' Williams claims that these approaches are used 'one on top of the other, one scene very tonal, very literal, very concrete, and the other music totally abstract and disassociated in the way the intervals relate to each other' (Bouzereau, 1997). As Lerner observes, however:

The music shifts stylistically from cues with a pointed lack of melody early in the film (emulating...Ligetti and Penderecki) to later cues featuring a clear, familiar melodic theme, harmonised with a post-Romantic tonal language. (2004: 102)

The score, as Lerner points out, thus sets up the more experimental musical style as strange, associating it with the aliens, but ultimately rejects the non-tonal in favour of the 'lovingly tonal and melodic...[B]y the final scenes in the film, Williams' music demands that we regard the extraterrestrials as not only benevolent but both familiar and familial' (ibid.) Not, it seems (based on the screenplay), what Spielberg originally had in mind as I discuss below.

First Contact

The final thirty plus minutes of *Close Encounters* – almost a quarter of the film

– is devoted to the UFO landing and first contact between mankind and the extraterrestrials. This sequence is the raison d'etre of *Close Encounters*, the operatic third act encounter between them and us that had been in Spielberg's mind from the very beginning. Spielberg had always envisaged it as a non-verbal 'experience', depicting what first contact might be like, what might take place and how it might feel to the people taking part. The resulting cornucopia of events is strange, beautiful, wondrous and awe-inspiring: the cavalcade of UFOS barnstorming the Devil's Tower in a wash of light and sound; the arrival of the giant Mothership that descends upon the mountain like a city of lights; the musical communication between Earth and extraterrestrial based around the (now iconic) five musical tones; the return of the missing World War Two pilots and other disappeared people (thereby resolving the mystery of Flight 19 set up in the opening scene); the emergence of the ETs themselves, and the subsequent first contact achieved using a system of hand signals originally devised by Zoltan Kodaly for communicating musical intervals to children.

The final sequence of *Close Encounters*, like 2001, aims to bypass 'verbal pigeonholing', and to try to render the whole visual experience into words would risk doing it an injustice. Therefore I shall confine myself to discussing the significance of the encounter that takes place between the humans and the aliens, with reference, in places, to the screenplay.

Before that, however, an analysis of *Close Encounters* would be incomplete without a little more discussion of the famous 'five tones' themselves: the way by which humans and extraterrestrials are shown to communicate in the film. The five tones, as already mentioned, have now, of course, become synonymous with *Close Encounters of the Third Kind*, iconic to it, in a similar way to how the two bass notes are iconic to Jaws (the musical conversation between the ARP synthesiser and the Mothership ends with those two bass notes in a form of homage!) In terms of narrative also, the five tones come into their own during the final encounter. As we know, Spielberg structured his story around mystery, and the five tones are akin to the Devil's Tower in this respect; we wait throughout the film for their significance to be revealed.

The use of the five tones originated as a solution to the problem of communication between interplanetary species; one of the reasons why the five tones remains such a powerful aspect of the film is because, as Morton points out, they acquire more and more meaning as the story goes on (1997: 82). Thematically they express the motif of 'communication across divides' introduced in the opening scene, where people of different nationalities struggle to communicate; and developed throughout the film in a number of variations, especially in the boundary-spanning character of Lacombe. It is fitting that Lacombe should be present both at the discovery of the five tones (in the India sequence), their interpretation (during the conference in which he demonstrates to delegates the Kodaly hand signs) and their final implementation in communicating both with the Mothership and the lone extraterrestrial at the climax of the film.

Moreover, Spielberg saw in the use of music as communication tool the commonality of technology and mathematics. Technology forms the medium between earthlings and extraterrestrials: the computerised ARP synthesiser (new technology in 1977) 'talks' to the superior technology of the Mothership through light, colour and sound; and as Spielberg himself says of mathematics:

> Mathematics is another way of communicating…but mathematics is also music. (Bouzereau, 1997)

In *Close Encounters*, Spielberg emphasises the teacher/pupil relationship of the extraterrestrials and earthlings; we have, it seems, learned enough musical vocabulary to be able to initiate communication but what the Mothership actually teaches us in response during the jam session with the ARP synthesiser, remains a mystery. However, there is little doubt that it is, as one character points out, our 'first day of school'.

As to the memorability of the five tones (not surprisingly they have since become a popular ringtone), Spielberg had not wanted a melody but a 'doorbell' announcing the presence of the aliens throughout the film, a prelude to first contact. Williams worked out mathematically that five tones would represent more than a musical fragment but not quite a melody; seven tones would be too much, four not enough. The final five tone sequence that he and Spielberg picked, from hundreds of variations, has particular resonance because it ends on a dominant note – the note from which resolution takes place. As Morton points out, by leaving the musical sequence unresolved, Spielberg and Williams create great anticipation: we are waiting for a response to the greeting, a reply to 'hello' (1997: 148).

Powerful though the five tones, the subsequent musical jam session and lightshow are, the supreme moment in the final sequence of *Close Encounters* occurs with the emergence of the extraterrestrials themselves. Spielberg deliberately obscures our view of the aliens through intense backlighting, keeping them strange and otherworldly. As Lacombe and Neary stand in front of the Mothership, its giant hatch opens, emitting piercing white light. A spiderlike head and torso emerges, tentatively at first. The Mayflower Project's team leader (played by Merrill Connally) steps forward slowly to greet the strange creature, who fully reveals itself, spreading its spindly arms outwards in a peaceful gesture (interpreted as Christ-like by numerous critics). Williams' score is suitably atonal, signalling the creature's strangeness. Lerner suggests that Penderecki's 'Threnody to the Victims of Hiroshima' may have served as a temp track for various sequences in *Close Encounters*; Williams uses strings in a similar way to create dissonance, evoking fear, but also awe, and ultimately a sense of the sublime.

The ETs are presented not as cuddly and a bit squidgy as they would be in many 1980s science fiction films. They are misshapen, bulbous-headed and foetal. Carl Rambaldi's design of the final alien who communicates with Lacombe is reminiscent of his creature in Zulawski's *Possession* (1981). They are resolutely 'Other', and *Close Encounters* celebrates their alterity. In the words of Elana Gomel, 'the radical Otherness of the universe' is revealed in this moment, and the encounter with the ontological Other is transformative (2014: 28, 4).

Spielberg places great emphasis on the differing reactions of the human scientists and technicians to the revelation of the ETs. Some cannot deal with it and back away; others step forward as if to embrace the experience. The screenplay indicates that 'this is both beautiful and disturbing to watch'.

We cut to inside a makeshift church chapel where the red-suited pilgrims are preparing to board the Mothership. A priest prays for their safety, whilst the astronauts look around nervously, distracted by the events taking place outside. Douglas Cowan argues that the scene – despite its blatantly Christian tone – serves to point out 'how limited...are our terrestrial religious notions' (2010: 88). Although many commentators insist that *Close Encounters* should be read as an explicit Christian allegory, this scene, according to Cowan seems to reject such a reading. Indeed, in the shooting draft screenplay (May, 1976), Spielberg includes a passage that supports Cowan's conclusion. As Roy is invited on board the Mothership by the aliens (and the script makes it clear that only he, and not the other astronauts, is allowed to embark), three ETs pass by the frightened priest who is on his knees genuflecting the salvation of the astronauts: 'Three tiny occupants can be seen just beyond him imitating his every pious gesture in perfect unison'.

This gently mocking moment is followed by the ETs actively blocking the other astronauts from entering the Mothership. In the screenplay, Roy hears in his mind Jiminy Crickett singing *When You Wish Upon A Star*, but there is an accompanying sense of irony. Roy shakes his head, not understanding why he is the only one deemed worthy. In a speech that seems to have been inspired by the writings of UFOlogist Aimé Michel, Lacombe tells Neary:

LACOMBE

We cannot pretend to understand all that is happening or about to happen.

It is a festival of the absurd.

And you must be receptive to it, innocent of it, and like a child in your openness and behaviour...

Too didactic a moment to be included in the final film perhaps, but it is one that is sorely missed. It clarifies the film's child analogy, but also, in describing (and depicting) the events as absurd, it refuses a celebration of similitude between human and extraterrestrial. It is impossible to interpret the aliens and their culture as familiar and familial. We must accept their strangeness, as must Roy.

After a preview of *Close Encounters* in 1978 Spielberg told press:

At first I wanted to indicate more than a physical exchange, but there's such a thing as crossing the boundary of reality. What we show can be accepted as real. If we'd gone much further, there was a danger of slipping into surrealism or just plain nonsense. I got what I wanted: Man's first contact with an extraterrestrial is formal, gentle, and a little strange. (Ebert, 1977)

This is a difficult balance to achieve, perhaps. The Williams score threatens to undercut Spielberg's original scripted intention in the next section as the romantic music swells into an orchestral version of *When You Wish Upon a Star*. Roy prepares to board the Mothership. He appears to need permission from his surrogate family to leave them behind, and turns to look at Jillian and Barry. Jillian, tearfully, nods her consent. This is perhaps Spielberg again mixing sincerity with cynicism, providing the audience with a tear-jerking grand finale.

Thankfully, Spielberg saves it at the final moment. The music dies away. Neary is left standing by himself, as if free to make up his own mind. As he walks up the ramp to board the Mothership alone, far from being a man who has abandoned his family to become a born-again child, he carries, as ambassador to other worlds, perhaps the greatest responsibility of all human beings.

Lacombe uses Kodaly hand signs to greet the ET.

4. *Close Encounters*: Cultural Impact

> The effect on society of discovering extraterrestrial intelligence might be as profound and long lasting as when Copernicus displaced the Earth from the Centre of the Universe. – S.E.T.I. Institute

During the filming of *Close Encounters*, a rumour spread that the film was being secretly sponsored by an American government agency as part of its acclimation programme to ready humankind for imminent first contact with extraterrestrials: 'part of the necessary training that the human race must go through in order to accept an actual landing,'(Balaban, 1978: 110). Such rumours are, as Balaban notes, like ghost stories at camp, concocted by UFO cults (Morton, 2007: 302) or perhaps Columbia's hyperactive marketing department: a good old fashioned urban myth (like the one about Stanley Kubrick 'directing' the fake Apollo moon landings). In some ways, however, there *is* a sense – conspiracy theories aside – that Spielberg may have achieved something along those lines. As J.P. Telotte wrote of *Close Encounters*, it's a film that 'takes us to and beyond certain perceptual and epistemological limits, moves us into unfamiliar "states"… if we can but go armed with this vision, we might, like Roy Neary, no longer feel quite so "lost"' (2001: 142). As such, the cosmic outlook of *Close Encounters* has influenced not only subsequent science fiction films but also the continuing fascination with extraterrestrial life and a whole UFO subculture. Even if the film itself is all but forgotten in certain quarters, its impact can still be keenly felt on popular culture and in the SETI/UFOlogy community at large.

Its impact in box office terms alone is huge. *Close Encounters* grossed over $116 million in America on its initial release in 1977 (and the *Special Edition* a further $15 million in 1980), placing it within the Top 10 grossing films of the 1970s. Vilmos Zsigmond won an Oscar for Best Cinematography; Frank Warner won a Special Achievement Award for Best Sound Editing; Joe Alves won a BAFTA for Best Production Design and John Williams a Grammy for his Soundtrack Album. The film's success, together with that of *Star Wars*, helped to usher in a new era of Science Fiction film: *Superman: The Movie* (1978), *Battlestar Galactica* (1978), *Alien* (1979), *Star Trek: The Motion Picture* (1979), Disney's *The Black Hole* (1979).

Its influence on American culture was immediate. The film was referenced and parodied in cartoons, magazine columns, chat shows and movies. Cubby Broccoli was one of the first movie producers to capitalise on the popularity of *Star Wars* and *Close Encounters* in the James Bond film *Moonraker* (1979), which included a direct reference to the now-famous five tones. Pop culture satire magazine *Mad* spoofed *Close Encounters* in its July 1978 issue (as 'Clod Encounters of the Absurd Kind'); it was satirised in popular TV comedy series *Happy Days* ('My Favourite Orkan', Season 5, episode 22, Feb. 1978) and the classic late night sketch show *Saturday Night Live* (May, 1978.) The film's title was parodied endlessly in such TV shows as the *Muppets, Alice, All in the Family, The Carol Burnett Show, Mork and Mindy, Sesame Street* and *Saturday Night Live*; in Hong Kong martial arts movie *Close Encounters of the Spooky Kind* (1980); a number of soft-core porn films including the Italian *Very Close Encounters of the Fourth Kind* (1978); and more recent sci-fi horror films and TV shows, *Grave Encounters* (2011), *Close Encounters* (2014, TV series), and *Continuum* ('Two Close Encounters', Season 1, Episode 6, March, 2012).

The release of *Close Encounters* also saw a dramatic increase in reported UFO sightings, although these were not new cases as one might expect, but older reports made by people who had previously been afraid to come forward, suggesting that the film had helped to raise public consciousness on the subject of UFOs. '"It is making it easier for people to talk about UFOs", J. Allen Hynek commented on the film in 1978, "UFOs have always been such a controversial subject. In fact in some cases one couldn't use the word UFO in polite society...People will now be far less embarrassed to say they have had a UFO experience"' (Beckley, 1978: 34).

In 1998 *The American Film Institute* polled more than 1500 critics and filmmakers to list the *100 Best American Movies* from the last 100 years. *Close Encounters* was voted number 64. Ten years later, it fell off the list, replaced by *Saving Private Ryan* as Spielberg's fifth film on the register, marking Spielberg as the director with the most films included (with *Jaws, Raiders of the Lost Ark, ET*, and *Schindler's List* as the other four), indicating that *Close Encounters* may have lost some of its popular appeal, historical significance and cultural importance – at least as far as Hollywood is concerned. (In an interview conducted in 2013, Joe Alves agreed that the film had become 'a forgotten movie, pretty much' [Awalt, 2013]. But even as it relinquished its place in the pantheon of the Hollywood mainstream, the past fifteen years have seen *Close Encounters* (coinciding with the DVD releases of its various versions, culminating in the Blu-Ray three-disc Thirtieth Anniversary 'Ultimate Edition' of all three cuts in 2007) grow in cult status among grassroots sci-fi fans. In 2011, *The Guardian* voted *Close Encounters* number eleven in their poll of the *Top 25 Sci-Fi and Fantasy Films of All Time* (with *2001: A Space Odyssey* at number one). That year, journalist Jonathan Jones, writing in the same newspaper, described *Close Encounters* as the first postmodern science fiction film (*The Guardian*, September 5th, 2011). Joss Whedon, in 2012, joined such other directors as Edgar Wright and J.J. Abrams in paying homage to the film, describing in interview how *Close Encounters* 'made me an existentialist' (*The Guardian*, April 15, 2012). In 2014 *Time Out* polled 'leading sci-fi experts, filmmakers, science fiction writers, film critics and scientists' to pick the *100 Best Sci-Fi Films Ever Made*. *Close Encounters* came in at number four. Amongst those who included the film in their lists were directors Bong Joon-Ho, Gareth Edwards, Guillermo Del Toro, Roland Emmerich and Stephen Hopkins. That same year *The British Film Institute* featured *Close Encounters* prominently in its film season, *Sci-Fi: Days of Fear and Wonder*. BFI National Archive curator John Oliver waxed nostalgically online ('Why I Love... Close Encounters of the Third Kind', bfi.org. uk, December 16th, 2014) about attending the film 'at least four times in the two weeks' that it screened at his local Newcastle-Upon-Tyne Odeon on its first release in Britain in March 1978 – a reminiscence that mirrors my own (substitute Nottingham for Newcastle in my case).

Its influence can be seen in numerous films that explore the notion of alien encounters. *The X Files* (1998), adapted from the phenomenally popular television series, saw FBI agents Mulder and Sully investigating a *Close Encounters*-like government conspiracy to hide the truth about extraterrestrials colonising the Earth since prehistoric times. The agents follow the mystery to Antarctica where aliens and a giant spaceship are found preserved beneath the ice.

The sci-fi/ home invasion horror *Dark Skies* (2013 – not to be confused with the short-lived television series of the same name) borrowed liberally from *Close Encounters* in its depiction of family menaced in their suburban home by sinister 'greys' intent on stealing their children (for what purpose is not clear). Scott Stewart's film fuses the Spielbergian suburban fantasy of *E.T.* with the suburban nightmare of *Poltergeist* (1982).

M. Night Shyamalan also took inspiration from *Close Encounters* (particularly the 'abduction of Barry' scene) for *Signs* (2002), a claustrophobic science fiction thriller with religious overtones, concerning a former Episcopal priest (played by Mel Gibson) who becomes convinced that his farm is being targeted by extraterrestrials. The film climaxes in an alien siege on the farmhouse, in which the lapsed priest experiences transcendence of a sort and regains his faith as a result.

Robert Zemeckis adapted *Contact* (1997) from Carl Sagan's novel, an ambitious exploration of the intersection between science, religion and alien contact. Jodie Foster plays a SETI scientist who detects a signal apparently transmitted from the 'Harp' star, Vega. The signal contains instructions on how to build a machine that apparently transports Foster through a wormhole into another dimension where she makes first contact with an extraterrestrial who takes the form of her deceased father.

On a somewhat lighter note, Simon Pegg and Nick Frost paid affectionate homage to Spielberg, *Close Encounters* and 60 years of alien conspiracy theories in *Paul* (2011). Two geeky sci-fi fans (played by Pegg and Frost) encounter a puckish grey named 'Paul' (Seth Rogen) while cruising the Extraterrestrial Highway near Area 51 in Nevada. Pursued by secret service agents, the unlikely trio end up at Devil's Tower, where 'Paul' is collected by spaceship having grown tired of his sojourn on Earth at a top secret military base (where he has been influencing popular culture ever since). Along the way they stop to pick up a middle aged woman whose dog was abducted by aliens years before; although played by Blythe Danner, the character is clearly based on Jillian Guiler in *Close Encounters*, and she gets to board the Mothership this time around. Spielberg has a voice cameo in the film, as himself, heard in a phone call with 'Paul' soliciting ideas for E.T.

In more general terms, the influence of *Close Encounters* extends to the 'intelligent' science fiction of such films as *Solaris* (2002), *Sunshine* (2007), *Oblivion* (2013), *Gravity* (2013) and, in particular, Christopher Nolan's *Interstellar* (2014), which tells the story of a team of astronauts who travel through a wormhole in search of a new planet for humans to inhabit, following the imminent demise of the Earth to environmental devastation. Spielberg had originally been attached to direct; Nolan rewrote the script to reflect his own concerns, but Spielbergian themes of family and fatherhood remain, and the central character (played by Matthew McConaughey) is portrayed as a Roy Neary-like everyman (albeit one who is a former pilot and NASA astronaut).

Equally significantly, the cultural influence of Close Encounters can be seen in continuing academic discourse within the social sciences concerning alien encounters and posthumanism. In his book *Alien Chic* (2004), Neil Badmington explores the possibility that the cultural obsession with alien gadgetry and stories of abduction stems from the need to reaffirm a sense of what is human in an age where science and technology continually blurs the boundaries between human and non-human. *Close Encounters* marks an important stepping stone between 'hating' the alien (as did the sci-fi films of the 1950s) and 'loving' it, even if, as Badmington asserts, *Close Encounters* ensures a humanist view by continuing to 'reinscribe the border between the human and the extraterrestrial' (89): a boundary that would become increasingly transgressed in the 1990s with *The X-Files* television series and films such as *Alien Resurrection* (1997).

Loving the Alien: Spielberg gives Rambaldi's Puck a kiss.

Elana Gomel argues in her book *Science Fiction, Alien Encounters, and the Ethics of Posthumanism* that posthumanism requires a new form of ethics, one 'predicated on the transformative encounter with the ontological other' (2014: 4). Ethics and the politics of human rights based on the Golden Rule (that we treat others only as we consent to being treated in the same situation) are, according to Gomel, inadequate in the age of posthumanism. Instead, she posits that posthumanism requires an 'ethics of transformation in which the encounter with the Other remakes the human subject'. Gomel contends that the aliens of science fiction film and literature are meaningful to us precisely because they provide a testing-ground for the ontological, epistemological and especially ethical issues raised by the possibility of the existence of alien intelligence – 'entities that defy our cultural and psychological conflation of reason and humanity'. Put simply, in the age of posthumanism, 'we need aliens because we are already alien to ourselves' (ibid).

It is perhaps in this context that *Close Encounters* is most significant. Science fiction cinema addressing alien contact post-9/11 can be seen in many ways as a return to the paranoia of the 1950s Cold War flying saucer movie. *Dark Skies*, *Signs*, et al portray extraterrestrial forces as sinister and menacing, hybridising sci-fi with horror in a similar way to such earlier classics as *Invaders from Mars* and *Invasion of the Body Snatchers*. However, this hybrid also highlights subtle but interesting differences between the two genres, particularly in relationship to the alien/monster. Both the alien (in sci-fi) and monster (in horror) represent 'Otherness'; a concept that can easily be lent a positive slant in sci-fi but is more problematic in horror, where the monster is necessarily portrayed negatively or – at best – ambiguously. It has been said that in the more progressive horror text, that which interrogates the relationship between the monster and its binary opposite, 'normality', the monster is ultimately recognised as *us* – those elements of ourselves that as a society we cast off or repress, projected onto the 'Other' as sinful, evil and degenerate; recognition of these aspects of ourselves thereby forces a re-evaluation of what we consider 'normal' and a potential reconciliation between ourselves and society's monsters (Wood, 2003, etc.) In science fiction films such as *2001* and *Close Encounters* – films that we might consider 'progressive' in so far as Otherness ultimately has a positive connotation (and even some sci-fi-horror films such as, for example, *Alien*, contain elements of this) – the alien, by contrast, is recognised as distinctly *not us*: therefore, rather than *similitude* it is *difference* that is highlighted in sci-fi, and which can potentially effect a radical transformation within us.

Spielberg did, of course, make his own science fiction-horror film in *War of the Worlds*, in which the extraterrestrials are recast, as in the H.G. Wells original, as merciless invaders harvesting human beings to fuel their killing machines, the tripods. In this way we might see *War of the Worlds* as a total inversion of *Close Encounters*, excepting that, as producer Kathleen Kennedy remarks:

> If you were to look at this as a trilogy of work by Steven, going from *Close Encounters* to *E.T.* and *War of the Worlds*, inherent in the idea of something unknown coming from outer space and what our reaction would be to that, I think the edgier, darker story has always been in there. (Bouzereau, 'We Are Not Alone', 2005)

These darker, edgier aspects only hinted at in *Close Encounters* (but there nonetheless) which come to the fore in *War of the Worlds* may be partly seen as a response to the catastrophe of 9/11, as Spielberg claims:

> *War of the Worlds* reflects 9/11 fears but it also reflects another impulse that we really are human beings and that we do come together to help each other survive, especially when we have a common enemy. (Bouzereau, 'Revisiting the Invasion', 2005)

However, at its heart, *War of the Worlds* represents, by and large, a return to the political conservatism of 50s alien invaders sci-fi, and is a reflection of Spielberg's changing philosophical viewpoints after *Close Encounters*. Spielberg, by his own admission, is no longer the optimist he was in 1977; indeed, his films since *Schindler's List* reflect profound despair at the human condition, at mankind's capacity for genocide (allegorised in *War of the Worlds* as the Martian invasion), and its corollary of survival-at-any-costs. Paula Wagner (executive producer of *War of the Worlds*) seems more on the mark when she comments of the film:

> It's a cautionary tale in a way. We're far more dangerous to ourselves than the extraterrestrial invaders. (ibid.)

Survival, in *War of the Worlds*, is less a matter of wider co-operative social endeavour (as Spielberg claims in the above quote), than a need to protect oneself – and, crucially, one's family – against 'a common enemy' by any means necessary. The romanticised paternalism of Schindler (Liam Neeson) is thus replayed in *War of the Worlds* with deeper reactionary inflection, as the Tom Cruise character discovers within himself a capacity for violence as a means of survival. He is ultimately willing to go to any lengths to protect his family – including the murder of another man; this is shown as regrettable but wholly necessary.

Of course, what Spielberg is sanctioning in the film is not violence *per se*. Rather it is the sanctity of family that Spielberg champions above all else, something that has come to replace *Close Encounters*' advocation of cosmic open-mindedness as Spielberg's project in his later films. At the root of Spielberg's concern lies the fear that the sanctity of family will be violated by external forces. This scenario (elements of it already existed in *Jaws*) has been played out with extraordinary consistency in his films after *Close Encounters*, be it in the destruction of family and home by Martians in *War of the Worlds*, the invasion of privacy by technology and corresponding violation of the family structures in *AI: Artificial Intelligence* and *Minority Report*, or the threat to family by the devastations of war (*Saving Private Ryan*, *War Horse*) or government sponsored terrorism (*Munich*). For Spielberg, only the strength of family bonds enables such adversity to be overcome and these threats to be vanquished or at least assuaged.

Close Encounters, then, when considered in an auteurist context seems to stand *outside* of Spielberg's oeuvre in many respects – or at least, the artist and his work have diverged significantly in the years since *Close Encounters* was made. 'I was a real devotee of the UFO phenomenon in the 1970s', Spielberg remarked in 2007, 'but since then, I've revised my thinking. With all the video cameras in the world today, why have sightings diminished?' But even if Spielberg now sees in his film only the 'blind optimism' of his youth, the philosophy behind *Close Encounters* – the belief that life exists elsewhere – continues in the scientific community, as evidenced by the Search for Extraterrestrial Intelligence.

Conclusion: We Are Not Alone

In the intervening years since the release of *Close Encounters* we can arguably see in the convergence of science fiction, UFOlogy and SETI, a continuing desire for the kind of transformative 'encounter' with alien intelligence that *Close Encounters* represents. The cultural impact of *Close Encounters* and 'transcendent' science fiction in general has, in fact, served to increase public awareness of the work being done in the scientific community to detect extraterrestrial life. Even now, as I write these final words, cosmologists involved in S.E.T.I. are proposing a more active form of search for alien civilisations, in which radio signals will be aimed at parts of the galaxy where Earth-like planets exist and with it an increased possibility of contact with intelligent life. Up until now, we have merely monitored the skies for radio signals from the outer spheres, without sending out signals of our own. However, the recent detection of these Earth-like planets (such as Kepler 186f) that may be capable of sustaining life in the 'habitable zones' of distant stars has prompted scientists to consider stepping up activities to what is known as M.E.T.I. – Messaging to Extraterrestrial Intelligence.

Naturally there are those, even now, who feel that such actions would be foolish: who can tell what the response of an alien civilisation may be to such messages (even if such a civilisation has the technology to travel the vast distances of space to invade our planet)? J. Allen Hynek would, no doubt, call such nay-saying symptomatic of a continuing 'cosmic provincialism' that lingers in some areas of the scientific establishment. After all, Stanley Kubrick pointed out back in 1968 that such fears are illogical, irrelevant (we have, after all, been unintentionally sending radio signals to outer space for decades): 'If others don't contact us, we must contact them,' remarked Kubrick; 'it's our destiny' (Nordern, 1968: 54).

Regardless of the objections of some scientists to M.E.T.I., the scientific community in general seems to be in consensus that the likelihood of intelligent life existing elsewhere is high (the so-called 'Drake Equation'), even though the probability of detection may be low. In 1991 and 1992, in recognition that the discovery of an extraterrestrial radio signal could occur 'at any time', the S.E.T.I. Institute gathered a team of specialists in history, theology, anthropology, psychology, sociology, international law, relations and theory, political science, the media and education to discuss the implications of S.E.T.I. for society. It was agreed that such a discovery would provide a welcome wake-up call for humanity: 'We need extraterrestrial civilisations to introduce us to an array of possibilities and variations beyond our past experience and also to shock us out of such parochialisms as regarding ourselves as the summit and final goal of evolution' (Finney, 2000: 141). In 1990, a Post-Detection Protocol was agreed amongst S.E.T.I. scientists, and sanctioned by the United Nations, stipulating that in the event of extraterrestrial life being detected, confirmation of it 'should be disseminated promptly, openly, and widely through scientific channels and public media' (S.E.T.I. Institute website, www.seti.org). It is like a moment straight out of *Close Encounters*, and speaks to the profound significance that such a discovery would represent for mankind, a discovery that, as Spielberg so vividly and unforgettably illustrates in his movie, 'would eclipse all other discoveries in history' (ibid.)

And that is why *Close Encounters of the Third Kind* remains a singular science fiction film. It marks the beginning of an emergence from an entrenched isolationist viewpoint of the Cold War, and looks forward to a new epoch in mankind's evolution. In so doing, it asks vital questions about our place in the cosmos.

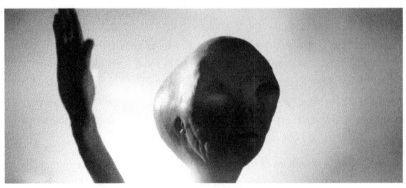

'*We Are Not Alone.*'

Works Cited

Alcott, Todd. 'Movie Night With Urbaniak: Close Encounters of the Third Kind.' http://toddalcott.livejournal.com/116391.html

Awalt, Steven. 'Interview: Joe Alves on Close Encounters', April 10, 2013. http://stevenawalt.com/?p=261

Bacher, Lutz. *The Mobile Mise-En-Scène: A Critical Analysis of the Theory and Practice of Long-Take Camera Movement in the Narrative Film*. New York: Arno Press, 1978.

Balaban, Bob. *Close Encounters of the Third Kind Diary*, New York: Paradise Press, 1978.

Balio, Tino. *The American Film Industry: Revised Edition*. Madison: University of Wisconsin Press, 1985.

Beckley, Timothy Green. 'Dr J Allen Hynek: From Harvard to Hollywood.' *Close Encounters of the Third Kind – The Fully Authorized Story*. New York: Paradise Press, 1978.

Booker, M. Keith. *Alternate Americas: Science Fiction Film and American Culture*. Westport, CT: Praeger, 2006.

Boorman, John. *Money into Light*. London: Faber, 1985.

Bordwell, David and Kristin Thompson. 'Reflections in a Crystal Eye'. June 4, 2008. *Observations on Film Art*. http://www.davidbordwell.net/blog/2008/06/04/reflections-in-a-crystal-eye/

Bouzereau, Laurent. *The Making of Close Encounters*. Columbia TriStar Home Entertainment, 1998.

_____. 'Revisiting The Invasion'. *War of the Worlds*. Paramount Pictures, 2005

_____. 'We Are Not Alone'. *War of the Worlds*. Paramount Pictures, 2005

_____. *Steven Spielberg: 30 Years of Close Encounters*. Sony Home Entertainment, 2007.

Britton, Andrew. *Britton on Film: The Complete Film Criticism of Andrew Britton*. Detroit: Wayne State University Press, 2009.

Brody, Richard. Steven Spielberg's Counterlife. *The New Yorker*, March 5, 2012. http://www.newyorker.com/culture/richard-brody/steven-spielbergs-counterlife

Buckland, Warren. *Directed by Steven Spielberg: Poetics of the Contemporary Hollywood Blockbuster*. New York: Continuum, 2006.

Buhl, Paul and Dave Wagner. *Hide in Plain Sight: The Hollywood Blacklistees in Film and Television, 1950 – 2002*. Houndmills, Basingstoke, Hants: Palgrave McMillan, 2005.

Byron, Stuart. 'The Searchers: Cult Movie of the New Hollywood.' *New York Magazine*, March 5, 1979, 45-48

Canby, Vincent. 'Movie Review: Close Encounters of the Third Kind.' *New York Times*, November, 17, 1977.

Columbia Pictures, *Close Encounters of the Third Kind Pressbook*, 1977.

Combs, Richard. 'Primal Scream: An Interview with Steven Spielberg'. *Sight and Sound* (Spring, 1977). Reprinted in *Steven Spielberg: Interviews*. Eds. Lester D. Friedman and Brent Notbohm. Jackson: University of Mississippi Press, 2000, 30-36.

Cousins, Mark. *The Story of Film: an Odyssey*, Network Releasing/BFI, 2001.

Cowan, Douglas E. *Sacred Space: The Quest for Transcendence in Science Fiction Film and Television*. Waco, Tx: Baylor University Press, 2010.

Crawley, Tony. 'The Steven Spielberg Story'. *Starburst* 53, January 1983, 28-34.

Cristol, Jonathan. 'Liberalism.' *Oxford Index* (March, 2011). http://oxfordindex.oup.com/view/10.1093/obo/9780199743292-0060

DeBaecque, Antoine and Serge Toubiana. *Truffaut: A Biography*. Berkeley: University of California Press, 1999.

Doherty, Thomas. *Teenager and Teenpics: The Juvenilization of American Movies in the 1950s*. Philadelphia: Temple University Press, 2002.

Ebert, Roger. 'Preview: Close Encounters of the Third Kind'. *Roger Ebert's Journal*. http://www.rogerebert.com/rogers-journal/preview-close-encounters-of-the-third-kind

Engel, Charlene. 'Language and the Music of the Spheres: Steven Spielberg's Close Encounters of the Third Kind.' *The Films of Steven Spielberg: Critical Essays*. Ed. Charles L.P. Silet. Lanham, Md: Scarecrow Press, 2002, 47-56.

Entman, Robert and Francis Seymour. 'Close Encounters with the Third Reich.' *Jump Cut* 18 (August 1978), 3-6.

Farber, Stephen. 'Close Encounters: Smooth Takeoff, Bumpy Landing.' *New West*, December 5, 1977. 26-27.

Finney, Ben. 'SETI, Consilience and the Unity of Knowledge'. *When SETI Succeeds: The Impact of High Information Contact*. Ed. Allen Tough. Bellevue, Wa: Foundation for the Future, 2000, 139-144.

Freer, Ian. *The Complete Spielberg*. London: Virgin Publishing, 2001, 60-76.

Glaessner, Verina. 'The Parallax View.' *Time Out Film Guide* 1998. Ed. John Pym. London: Penguin, 1997, 651.

Gomel, Elana. *Science Fiction, Alien Encounters and the Ethics of Posthumanism: Beyond the Golden Rule*. Houndmills, Basingstoke: Palgrave McMillan, 2014.

Gomery, Douglas. *The Hollywood Studio System: A History*. London: BFI, 2005.

Gordon, Andrew M. 'Close Encounters: The Gospel According to Steven Spielberg'. *Literature/Film Quarterly* 8, no.3 (1980): 156-64.

_____. *Empire of Dreams: The Science Fiction and Fantasy Films of Steven Spielberg*. Lanham: Rowman and Littlefield, 2008.

Haskell, Molly. *From Reverence to Rape: The Treatment of Women in the Movies* (second edition). Chicago: University of Chicago Press, 1987.

Hodenfield, Chris. 'The Sky is Full of Questions: Science Fiction in Steven Spielberg's Suburbia.' *Rolling Stone*, January 26, 1978, 33-38.

Kendrick, James. *Darkness in the Bliss-Out: A Reconsideration of the Films of Steven Spielberg*. London: Bloomsbury, 2014.

King, Geoff and Tanya Krzywinska. *Science Fiction Cinema: From Outerspace to Cyberspace*. London: Wallflower Press, 2000.

Kroll, Jack. 'The UFOs are Coming!' *Newsweek*, November 21, 1977. 88-92.

Laycock, Joseph. 'The Folk Piety of William Peter Blatty: The Exorcist in the Context of Secularization,' *Interdisciplinary Journal of Research on Religion* 5 (2009): 2-27.

Lerner, Neil. 'Nostalgia, Masculinist Discourse and Authoritarianism in John Williams' scores for Star Wars and Close Encounters of the Third Kind.' *Off the Planet: Music, Sound and Science Fiction Cinema*. Ed. Philip Hayward. New Barnet: John Libbey, 2004, 96-108.

Mackay-Kallis, Susan. *The Hero and the Perennial Journey Home in American Film*. Philadelphia: University of Pennsylvania Press, 2001.

McBride, Joseph. *Steven Spielberg: A Biography*. London: Faber, 1997.

Maslow, Abraham H. (Ed. Ann R. Kaplan.) *The Maslow Business Reader*. New York: John Wiley, 2000.

Morris, Nigel. *The Cinema of Steven Spielberg: Empire of Light*. London: Wallflower Press, 2007.

Morton, Ray. *Close Encounters of the Third Kind: The Making of Steven Spielberg's Classic Film*. New York: Applause Theatre and Cinema Books, 2007.

Nordern, Eric. 'Playboy Interview: Stanley Kubrick'. *Playboy* (September, 1968). Reprinted in *Stanley Kubrick: Interviews*. Ed. Gene D. Phillips. Jackson: University of Mississippi Press, 2001, 47-74.

Pirie, David. 'A Prodigy Zooms In: A Child Cineaste Who Now Makes Movies and Money with Equal Facility. *Time-Out Interviews 1968-1998*. Ed. Frank Broughton. London: Penguin Books, 1998.

Plantinga, Carl. 'The Scene of Empathy and the Human Face on Film'. *Passionate*

Views: Film, Cognition, and Emotion. Eds. Carl Plantinga and Greg M.Smith. Baltimore: The Johns Hopkins University Press, 1999, 239-55.

Poster, Steve. 'The Mind Behind Close Encounters of the Third Kind'. *American Cinematographer*, February 1978. Reprinted in *Steven Spielberg: Interviews*. Eds. Lester D. Friedman and Brent Notbohm. Jackson: University of Mississippi Press, 2000, 55-69.

Rowley, Stephen. 'Steven Spielberg'. *Senses of Cinema* 38 (February, 2006). http://sensesofcinema.com/2006/great-directors/spielberg/

Royal, Susan. 'Steven Spielberg in His Adventures on Earth'. *American Premiere*, July 1982. Reprinted in *Steven Spielberg: Interviews*. Eds. Lester D. Friedman and Brent Notbohm. Jackson: University of Mississippi Press, 2000, 84-106.

Ruppersberg, Hugh. 'The Alien Messiah'. *Alien Zone: Cultural Theory and Contemporary Science Fiction Cinema*. Ed. Annette Kuhn. London: Verso, 1990, 32-38.

Sanders, John. *The Film Genre Book*. Leighton Buzzard: Auteur, 2009.

Schaeffer, Dennis and Larry Salvato. *Masters of Light: Conversations with Contemporary Cinematographers*. Berkeley: University of California, 1984.

Sharrett, Christopher, 'The Myth of Apocalypse and the Horror Film: The Primacy of Psycho and The Birds.' *Framing Hitchcock: Selected Essays from The Hitchcock Annual*. Eds. Sidney Gottlieb and Christopher Brookhouse. Detroit: Wayne State University Press, 2002. 355-372.

Scorsese, Martin. 'Confessions of a Movie Brat'. *Anatomy of the Movies*. Ed. David Pirie. London: Windward, 1981, 132-139.

Shaw, Tony. 'Negotiating the Cold War in Film: The Other Side of Hollywood's Cold War: Images of Dissent in the 1950s'. *American Visual Cultures*. Eds. Holloway, David and John Beck. London: Bloomsbury, 2005, 133-140.

Shay, Don. 'Steven Spielberg on Close Encounters.' *Cinefantastique*. Vol 7, No 3-4, 1978.

Sobchack, Vivian. *Screening Space: The American Science Fiction Film*. New

Brunswick, NJ: Rutgers University Press, 2004.

Spielberg, Steven and Leslie Waller. *Close Encounters of the Third Kind*. London: Sphere Books, 1978.

Sragow, Michael. 'A Conversation with Steven Spielberg'. *Rolling Stone*, July 22, 1982. Reprinted in *Steven Spielberg: Interviews*. Eds. Lester D. Friedman and Brent Notbohm. Jackson: University of Mississippi Press, 2000, 107-119.

Telotte, J.P. *Science Fiction Film*. Cambridge: Cambridge University Press, 2001.

Tuchman, Mitch. 'Close Encounter with Steven Spielberg.' *Film Comment* (January-February, 1978). Reprinted in *Steven Spielberg: Interviews*. Eds. Lester D. Friedman and Brent Notbohm. Jackson: University of Mississippi Press, 2000, 37-54.

Turnock, Julie A. *Plastic Reality: Special Effects, Technology, and the Emergence of 1970s Blockbuster Aesthetics*. New York: Columbia University Press, 2015.

Trumbull, Douglas. 'Statement by Douglas Trumbull'. January 11, 2012. http://douglastrumbull.com/videos

Vallee, Jacques. *The Invisible College: What a Group of Scientists Has Discovered about UFO Influences on the Human Race*. San Antonio, TX: Anomalist Books, 1975 (reprint 2014).

Van Wert, Bill. 'The Exorcist: Radical Therapy.' *Jump Cut*, no.1, 1974 4-5.

Vogler, Christopher. *The Writer's Journey: Mythic Structure for Storytellers and Screenwriters*. London: Boxtree, 1996.

Walsh, Roger and Frances Vaughan. 'On Transpersonal Definitions'. *Journal of Transpersonal Psychology*, 25 (2), 1993, 125-182.

Warren, Bill. *Keep Watching the Skies!: American Science Fiction Movies of the Fifties*. Jefferson, NC: McFarland & Co, 2010.

Wasser, Frederick. *Spielberg's America*. Oxford: John Wiley and Sons, 2013.

Watts, Steven. *The Magic Kingdom: Walt Disney and the American Way of Life*. Columbia: University of Missouri Press, 1997.

Williams, Raymond. 'Utopia and Science Fiction.' *Science Fiction: A Critical Guide*. Ed. Patrick Parrinder. Abingdon, Oxon: Routledge, 1979.

Williams, Tony. 'Close Encounters of the Authoritarian Kind'. *Wide Angle*, Vol 5. No.4 (1983): 22-29.

Wilson, Colin. *Mysteries: An Investigation into the Occult, the Paranormal and the Supernatural*. London: Grafton Books, 1979.

Wood, Robin. *Hollywood from Vietnam to Reagan...and Beyond*. New York: Columbia University Press, 2003.

ALSO AVAILABLE IN THIS SERIES

CONSTELLATIONS
studies in science fiction film and TV

BLADE RUNNER

Sean Redmond

CONSTELLATIONS
studies in science fiction film and TV

INCEPTION

David Carter

Printed and bound by CPI Group (UK) Ltd, Croydon, CR0 4YY

13/04/2025

14656581-0001